To Hope,

As your team .... meant everything to your life; and so it has for ours as well. Thank you for your skills; your Faith has been a shining light for us through some dark days. You were put into our lives by the Father, and gave us Hope.

In Him.

Jean Lee and Fred Lee

"As for the saints who are in the earth, They are the majestic ones in whom is all my delight."

Psalm 16:3 (NASB)

True-Life Short-Story Devotionals That Inspire

JEAN LEE

Living the Legacy

*Finding the Goodness of the Lord in
the Land of the Living*

WESTBOW
PRESS®
A DIVISION OF THOMAS NELSON
& ZONDERVAN

WestBow Press books may be ordered through booksellers or by contacting:

WestBow Press
A Division of Thomas Nelson & Zondervan
1663 Liberty Drive
Bloomington, IN 47403
www.westbowpress.com
1 (866) 928-1240

ISBN: 978-1-5127-0553-9 (sc)
ISBN: 978-1-5127-0554-6 (hc)
ISBN: 978-1-5127-0552-2 (e)

Library of Congress Control Number: 2015912158

Print information available on the last page.

WestBow Press rev. date: 08/20/2015

Contents

To My Husband

Our journey together began many years ago. Without you, most of these stories could not have been written. Thank you for your love and faithfulness in all things. To borrow Daddy's phrase, "You are the best on earth."

Irad W. Lee with his grandson, Irad W. Lee IV

I would have despaired unless I had believed that I would see the goodness of the LORD in the land of the living. (Psalm 27:13)

Preface

Growing up in a family of faith was quintessential to my love of God. My journey of faith provides the landscape for discovering God's presence in life's ordinary circumstances, giving us reassurance of His constant vigilance.

In our fast-paced lifestyles, the inspired Word of God provides power for living life as a child of the King.

Compiled in a series of true short stories, *Living the Legacy* is written in an easy-to-read, conversational style, with a Southern flavor. It can be used as a devotional or read in its entirety.

Regardless of whether you are a seeker, have lost your way, or desire to deepen your faith, you will be encouraged, inspired, and grow in faith through the bird's-eye view of moments in time chronicled within *Living the Legacy*. Some of the stories express emotions that challenge as we see that the Father weaves each thread of life experience into a beautiful tapestry.

The message within *Living the Legacy* is intended as a tribute to the Lord for surrounding us with the wonder of His beauty, for forgiving us, and for conveying His heritage as a child of the King—a heritage that begins on earth and continues in heaven.

My heart's desire is for all to come to the saving knowledge of Jesus Christ as Lord and to savor His Word as essential for living *His* legacy here and now.

"Now to Him who is able to keep you from stumbling, and to make you stand in the presence of His glory blameless with great joy, to the only God our Savior, through Jesus Christ our Lord, *be* glory, majesty, dominion and authority, before all time and now and forever. Amen" (Jude 1:24–25).

Jean Lee

Acknowledgments

With profound thanksgiving for the joys and tribulations of shared experiences with family, as related in each story in *Living the Legacy*, I am indebted— to my family for their love— and for every occasion that has caused me to increase my faith by seeking the Word of God. My heart is full to overflowing with love and gratitude for each one of you.

I convey my sincerest thanks to family and friends— faithful believers and lovers of the Lord—who encouraged me to publish. May the Father multiply your seed for sowing and increase the harvest of your righteousness.

To Lamont Fells and his colleagues at West Bow Press, I impart my deepest appreciation for your support and guidance.

Although the stories within recount the past, I look to the Lord with thanksgiving and great expectation for new tomorrows—opportunities to live *His* legacy and give glory, honor, and praise to Him.

> 'I will give thanks to the Lord with all my heart;
> I will tell of all Your wonders.' (Psalm 9:1)

"For this reason I bow my knees before the Father, from whom every family in heaven and on earth derives its name, that He would grant you, according to the riches of His glory, to be strengthened with power through His Spirit in the inner man, so that Christ may dwell in your hearts through faith" (Ephesians 3:14–17)

Introduction

Preceded by untold generations of family faithful who taught Jesus Christ as Lord, my parents, grandparents, aunts, and uncles advanced the witness of Christ.

My parents settled on their farm in East Tennessee in 1939, and worked the remainder of their lives fulfilling their dream by living their legacy of faith on the land.

Born into a family of five daughters, my sisters and I lived our formative years on the farm. Mama and Daddy nurtured and guided my sisters and me; and counseled and disciplined us as we grew.

I continue to live on a portion of the farm with the love of my life, my husband, Irad Lee.

From the outset of my marriage to Irad, the Lee family took me in as one of their own. My family and Irad's paint a beautiful portrait of life and love centered on the Lord.

Irad and I raised a son, Irad Lee III, and a daughter, Julia Lee Rogers. We now have six grandchildren as a blessing from the Lord, and so, the legacy continues.

Chronicled within are stories of everyday life events, the kind you may have experienced. It is my joy to introduce my family to you as I relate each story.

Most importantly, you will meet the Heavenly Father in the details, because every story leads to Him.

You will find reassurance in discovering that God is in step with the details of your daily life.

Every family is different. There are wonderful families; and some not so wonderful. You may know nothing about your biological family— or you may have loved and lost.

The Heavenly Father is intimately acquainted with you—and knows your needs, your hurts, and your heart's desire. God understands; and has experienced it all in His Son, Jesus—pain and suffering, rejection and loss, love and joy.

The Father yearns for you to know Him as He knows you—and to love Him *because* He loves you.

Need encouragement, comfort, and forgiveness? God can provide. Need guidance, protection, and love? He's got you covered!

If you are a believer in Jesus, He wants you to grow in grace. If you are seeking Him, the Father invites you to come home to His family— where you belong.

God chose you for a time like this.

He has given you a life to live. He desires for you to experience it in abundance—and embrace and live His legacy on earth now, and afterward, in heaven.

God's Dependability, Power, and Deliverance through Jesus

Faster than a speeding bullet, more powerful than a locomotive, able to leap tall buildings in a single bound. It's Superman!

Three descriptive phrases and we readily recognize him. Recognition is made easy because Superman is consistent. He never changes. He is powerful, fights evil, and rescues the helpless.

I have a favorite superhero. Descriptive phrases include:

- "The same yesterday, today and forever" (Hebrews 13:8).
- "Power is perfected in weakness" (2 Corinthians 12:9).
- "He rescued us from the domain of darkness" (Colossians 1:13).

Recognize Him?

It's the Lord Jesus.

Do you *know* Him?

Flyin' High

God's Instruction, Wisdom, Counsel, and Invitation

Never having been out of the Southeast, my husband, Irad, and I planned a trip to Acapulco, Mexico— a 1970s glamour destination. I was nervous yet excited about the trip. Our "home" that week was the Hyatt. Gorgeous bay-front views, sumptuous breakfasts, Hollywood-style pools; it was luxury.

From our balcony, we observed people experiencing a new adventure: parasailing. Every day Irad said he was going to give it a try. Toward the end of the week, almost out of time, my daredevil husband told me to pack a day bag. He had signed up!

When we arrived at the launch area, Irad was given instructions, and he 'suited up'. His turn was next, after the middle-aged female tourist finished. I remember thinking if that woman could do it, I knew without a doubt Irad would be safe!

We were standing near the group of men, parasail ride operators, who were assigned to shore duty and were responsible for 'landing' their human cargo. With video camera in hand and heart in my throat, we observed the woman's descent. The onshore staff became frantic upon her approach, and we surmised that something must be very wrong. With conflicting emotions—horror and humor—we watched as the woman began to bounce down the beach like a big beach ball, one, two, three, four times, with the men chasing her!

A close call, caused by failing to follow simple instructions and pull the cord. She appeared to be okay.

Not deterred, Irad was next. Amazing. He soared like an eagle high over buildings and bay, pulled the cord—perfect landing!

Life is an adventure. The Lord has given us simple instructions for a safe landing.

"You shall love the Lord your God with all your heart, and with all your soul, and with all your mind. This is the great and foremost commandment. The second is like it, 'You shall love your neighbor as yourself'" (Matthew 22:37–39).

In All Her Born Days

God's Forgiveness and Joyful Response to Repentance

January 15 is the birth date of our daughter, Julia. Memories of her birth are so clear—being told she was a girl (thought a boy), her first cry, naming her and dedicating her to the Lord while on the delivery table. The whole family celebrated her birth with tears and jubilation.

Equally unforgettable was her second birthday—not the one when she reached age two—her eternal birth, her day of redemption. On that day, the children's Sunday school class that Julia attended was half over. Irad and I were nearby in a couple's class of twenty. Julia came running through the door into our class, heedless of her interruption, tears streaming down her face, eyes searching the room until she found us. She cried out, declaring to many witnesses, "I want to be saved."

The date escapes me.

Jesus teaches of two births.

"Truly, truly, I say to you, unless one is born of water and the Spirit he cannot enter the kingdom of God. That which is born of the flesh is flesh, and that which is born of the Spirit is spirit" (John 3:5–6).

The date of Julia's birth into the family of God may be a lost memory in my recollections—but not the Father's. He does not forget birthdays. He celebrates in heaven.

"… I tell you, there is rejoicing in the presence of the angels of God over one sinner who repents" (Luke 15:10 NIV).

I Want to Hold Your Hand

God's Protection, Compassion, Care, and Deliverance

When March Madness comes along, basketball is in full swing. Basketball is a family thing. Daddy played basketball in the 1920s. Three generations followed him: his children, grandchildren, and greats!

My elder sisters played at the old gym at Madisonville High School.

There was a big game one evening. The gym was packed. That was the night I lost track of Mama and Daddy. I was six years old.

When the game ended, the crowd began moving out the worn double doors onto the sidewalk. A single street light lit the way in an otherwise inky dark night. Frightened and stuck in the middle of the crowd, I reached for Daddy's hand.

I knew immediately it was the hand of a stranger.

Daddy's hands were calloused and rough from the farm. The hand I held was smooth. I don't remember crying in the darkness, but assuredly, I did. The stranger knew our family and located Daddy.

Oh, what relief. I was once again safe, holding Daddy's hand.

He left for heaven in 1998—about March Madness time. I miss those beloved hands.

But there's another hand I rely on, the hand of my Savior. It's like Daddy's in many ways: scarred and calloused, comforting and safe, strong and sure—guiding me to safety.

"For I am the LORD your God who takes hold of your right hand and says to you, Do not fear, I will help you" (Isaiah 41:13 NIV).

Love at First Sight

God's Gentleness and His Love in Sending a Savior

Almost all families carefully name their children; it is a topic for dinner discussion and bedtime meditation.

The choosing of a name in advance of our fourth grandchild's birth in the year 2000 was no exception. Many names were considered, discarded, and reconsidered. The goal was to pick a unique name, preferably one selected from the Bible.

At our granddaughter's birth, she was named Rachel, a name recorded in the Word of God. Remember Jacob, Abraham's grandson? He was the husband of Rachel—a love-at-first-sight Bible story!

Yet, the distinctiveness of her name's meaning is the special part. Rachel means *ewe*, a female sheep.

Sheep—it is the term that the Bible prophets attribute to believers of Messiah.

"He will tend his flock like a shepherd; he will gather the lambs in his arms; he will carry them in his bosom, and gently lead those that are with young" (Isaiah 40:11 ESV).

Messiah, Jesus the Christ, the Son of God, is our Shepherd and Sacrifice, for He became the sacrificial lamb—innocent, without blemish.

"For you know that it was not with perishable things such as silver or gold that you were redeemed from the empty way of life handed down to you from your ancestors, but with the precious blood of Christ, a lamb without blemish or defect" (1 Peter 1:18–19 NIV).

Why did the Father sacrifice His only Son for the likes of us? The answer is simple. It was love at first sight—love and life given freely by God, from the beginning and throughout the eternal ages to come.

"This is how God showed his love among us: He sent his one and only Son into the world that we might live through him" (1 John 4:9 NIV).

Trading Places

God's Grace and His Acceptance of New Family Members

Car buying in our household occurs about every decade. My husband, Irad, and I have always gone car shopping together, except for one time.

That car-buying episode occurred in 1976. We were in need of another vehicle. Irad's brother, David had his car for sale. David's car was a good deal—priced right, reliable, stylish and chocolate brown. Irad purchased the car— without me!

I really tried to like the car, but *chocolate brown* had to go. Weeks later, the kids and I were in a neighboring town forty miles away. The town was renowned for its motor mile. Thinking I might indulge myself, I swung by the GM dealership. I spotted a car that I liked and took a closer look. I noticed a car salesman running toward us at breakneck speed. Escape was impossible.

As we pulled onto the highway to depart, our chocolate brown car was visible in the rearview mirror.

I hoped for Irad's approval but fretted over his reaction. With no cell phones in those days, there was no easy way to alert him that the kids and I were driving home a *different car* with the car salesman in tow!

My indulgent behavior could have become a family disaster, but thankfully did not. Irad was gracious as he drove the car *and* the car salesman forty miles back to the dealership and finalized the trade!

"Among them we too all formerly lived in the lusts of our flesh, indulging the desires of the flesh and of the mind, and were by nature children of wrath, even as the rest. But God, being rich in mercy, because of His great love with which He loved us, even when we were dead in our transgressions, made us alive together with Christ (by grace you have been saved)" (Ephesians 2:3–5)

Saved by grace—disaster avoided.

It is incomprehensible that the Lord God would want a child of wrath as one of His own. Yet He does.

"Therefore if anyone is in Christ, *he is* a new creature; the old things passed away; behold, new things have come" (2 Corinthians 5:17).

Trading old for new, wrath for righteousness. It's a great deal.

Make the trade!

The Tracks of His Tears

God's Love and Our Victory through His Sacrifice

Moving on up from a crib to a big boy's twin bed was an important step in the life of our oldest grandchild, Irad Lee IV. At three years, with a sense of joy and excitement, his little hands assisted Granddaddy in carrying the bed parts into the room and completing assembly.

It was a sleepover night at our house. No need to coax Irad IV to bed; he readily jumped in! Our bedtime routine included a Bible story. He had his favorites that were repeated many times—except for this night.

As I was turning the pages, his baby hands stopped mine at a color illustration of Jesus Christ—in agony, nailed to the cross.

With a troubled countenance, he pointed to Jesus and asked who he was and what had happened? Looking at the image of Jesus, explaining for a three-year-olds comprehension, I articulated God's plan of salvation.

My narrative went something like this.

> God the Father lives in heaven with His only child, Jesus.

> God loves us. He wants a big family— and desires to adopt us as His own.

However, we have a problem. Every single person on earth is born imperfect. The Bible calls it sin.

"For all have sinned, and come short of the glory of God" (Romans 3:23).

God sent His Son, Jesus, to live a perfect life on earth. He invites us to believe Jesus is His Son.

"For God so loved the world, that He gave His only begotten Son, that whoever believes in Him shall not perish, but have eternal life." (John 3:16)

Religious men did not believe Jesus was God's Son, so they whipped Jesus, nailed Him to the cross, and killed Him.

Jesus was buried in a tomb, but after three days, the power of God's glory brought Jesus back to life— called the resurrection.

God allowed these events to happen because Jesus *had* to die— so that we could live with Him; for "... the blood of Jesus His Son cleanses us from all sin." (1 John 1:7)

When we believe Jesus, our adoption into God's family to live with Him forever is a *sure thing*. (see Galatians 4:4-7)

Always remember, God's promises are true— for He cannot lie! (see Titus 1:2)

Glancing over at Irad IV to confirm his understanding, I witnessed his astonishing response. Huge tears were streaming down his face. It's certain that the Father was pleased with our little one.

Many times since that night of long ago, I have pondered Irad IV's reaction to the image of Jesus crucified. I have asked the Father to teach me to please Him as a child—to grieve when I remember Christ's agony, and to rejoice as I share His victory.

"but thanks be to God, who giveth us the victory through our Lord Jesus Christ" (1 Corinthians 15:57 ASV).

Splash

God's Forgiveness and Joyful Response for Repentance

Swimming was a joy when we were little. My twin sister, Dean, and I learned to swim in the Tellico River—lips blue and teeth chattering from the icy waters.

Then came the lazy, hazy, crazy days of summer in 1962, when we were twelve years old and swam like fish in the water.

The local Jaycees built a large swimming pool in Houston Park, equipped with a baby pool, springboard, and high dive. The admission was twenty-five cents.

The Jaycees faithfully opened the pool and concession every day. The sounds of that summer endure: Ray Charles crooning "I Can't Stop Loving You" over the loud speaker blended with the shrieks of laughter from friends showing off their latest water tricks. At age thirteen, Irad (my phone boyfriend at that time, and future husband) riding his moped, made occasional appearances at the fence to check out the action. It was a summer to remember.

Dean and I had to clean Mama's house before spending almost every afternoon at the pool. Dean cleaned the kitchen. I worked on the rest of the house. It was my task to come up with the money for pool admission. The best place to search for spare change was under the sofa cushions. Every night Daddy would stretch out on the sofa and every day I would search for the change that escaped his pockets. Coming up with fifty cents was victory, and more was an added bonus. We could buy a thirst-quenching ice-cold drink at the pool!

Reliving those times reminds me of another search for money. The gospel of Luke tells us of a woman searching for her lost coin.

"Or what woman, if she has ten silver coins and loses one coin, does not light a lamp and sweep the house and search carefully until she finds it? When she has found it, she calls together her friends and neighbors, saying, 'Rejoice with me, for I have found the coin which I had lost!' In the same way, I tell you, there is joy in the presence of the angels of God over one sinner who repents" (Luke 15:8–10).

Now that's a story of victory! And the drink bonus is forever free.

"but whoever drinks of the water that I will give him shall never thirst; but the water that I will give him will become in him a well of water springing up to eternal life" (John 4:14).

The Masters

God's Provision for Salvation in Christ and Blessing for Obedience

My husband, Irad, loves golf. He didn't begin playing until his late thirties. He knew that it would take practice to develop the technique, and he spent many afternoons on the golf course.

I too learned to love the sport and even tried to play. After many failed attempts, I decided that my best role was to caddy and to drive the golf cart.

One of Irad's dreams is to attend and view firsthand the ceremony and tradition of the Masters Tournament at Augusta National Golf Club. I would love to experience the beauty of the course. We are told that because of the preeminence and popularity of the tournament, tickets are expensive and hard to get.

The Masters Tournament is held every year in the spring. When play is finished, the tee flags are placed in the maintenance shed; the treasured green jacket is awarded to the winner. Only one can win.

There is another Master's tournament. It's played every minute of life. The Master provides the course, renewing it day by day. The course is not played with clubs—but actions, choices, and surrender.

Surrender: it sounds like defeat, waving a white flag. The opposite is true.

The Lord Jesus surrendered to an unspeakable beating. He was alone and abandoned by all.

It was a mob scene. Lies were told. Propaganda was advanced.

The crowds stood and watched an unjust trial, a gruesome beating, a horrible death.

Had we been standing on the roadside that day, would we have joined the chants of the crowd or cowered fearfully at the sight?

Jesus wore a crown that day—a crown of thorns.

We wouldn't call that victory, but it was. Victory was *won* for not just *one,* but for all people who decide to surrender.

No green jacket is awarded. That's a tawdry prize when compared to a crown—straight from the Master's hand.

"And every man that striveth for the mastery is temperate in all things. Now they do it to obtain a corruptible crown; but we an incorruptible" (1 Corinthians 9:25 KJV).

God's Response to Our Pleas for Holiness

If you grew up in rural America, you might remember the days of your youth—going to the county fair. Upon arrival, the air was filled with anticipation, excitement, and a distinctive scent—a curious combination of hay, cotton candy, and roasting hot dogs. Unforgettable. The colorful lights, music, and thrilling rides were an unmistakable invitation to enjoy the evening. There were sounds of laughter. And calls of workers hawking their wares, daring people to beat the odds by shooting moving ducks or knocking over bottles. Passersby heard shouts of *step right up!* The invitation was irresistible.

With eager faces, our children begged for spare change to make their attempt at winning a prize.

Those were the days when right living was respected and wrong choices were punished.

The Lord invites us to step right up and live right. The Bible calls it righteousness when one is filled by the Holy Spirit.

Most people yearn to live right. If the act of selflessness is to please God, then righteous living has been achieved. The ultimate act of righteousness is surrender.

The writer of the old hymn "I Surrender All" knew righteousness.

All to Jesus I surrender, All to Him I freely give;

I will ever love and trust Him, In His presence daily live.

All to Jesus I surrender, Humbly at His feet I bow,

Worldly pleasures all forsaken; Take me Jesus, take me now.

All to Jesus, I surrender, Lord I give myself to Thee;

Fill me with Thy love and power; Let Thy blessing fall on me.

All to Jesus, I surrender, Now I feel the sacred flame.

Oh, the joy of full salvation! Glory, glory, to His Name*!*

"Create in me a clean heart, O God, and renew a new and *right* spirit within me" (Psalm 51:10 KJV emphasis added).

Take the Bull by the Horns

God's Strength, Sanctuary, and Deliverance

Mama and Daddy built their dairy barn in the late 1930s. It was designed as a stanchion barn. It had all-concrete floors, with raised stalls. Metal bars divided each stall. The feed trough and walkway were in front of the cows' heads. Workers filled the troughs with feed.

All the cattle wore chains and had horns in those days and for many years following. At milk time, the cows were herded into the barn, filling each stanchion, and were chained. The bull came in with the cows and took the last stall.

In the 1950s, when my twin sister, Dean, and I were little girls, we were in the barn many times during milking.

Mama cautioned us about those horns.

It was frightening to use the walkway in front of the cows' heads. Their horns seemed so close.

I would plaster my body against the wall as I inched down the walk. Dean was very brave and walked confidently in front of the cows' heads and horns.

It was a day like any other, though the bull was restless. Daddy was about to chain him when disaster struck. The Jersey bull gored Daddy with his horns, throwing Daddy over his head, onto the concrete alley. Blood was everywhere.

I wanted to kill that bull.

And that's exactly what the Lord instructed in His Word.

"And thou shalt take of the blood of the bullock, and put it upon the horns of the altar with thy finger, and pour all the blood beside the bottom of the altar" (Exodus 29:12 KJV).

Horns—a symbol of strength and sanctuary. The altar was designed with four of them on each corner.

The verse describes the sanctuary of Jesus—His strength, His blood, His sacrifice for us.

Daddy was pierced in his side. So was Jesus.

"… one of the soldiers pierced Jesus' side with a spear, bringing a sudden flow of blood and water" (John 19:34 NIV).

Daddy lived to see another day, and so did Jesus for days eternal as the horn of salvation.

"Blessed *be* the Lord God of Israel, For He has visited us and accomplished redemption for His people, And has raised up a horn of salvation for us In the house of David His servant" (Luke 1:68–69).

God's Power to Transform Lives

The house is peaceful. Relaxation can begin. The baby is down for the night.

Parents everywhere can relate.

My husband, Irad, and I always breathed a sigh of relief when our firstborn active toddler went to sleep.

Our son, Irad Lee III was a very good baby. His crib was a traditional baby bed with bars and a foot release to lower the side. When the side was raised and clicked into place, he knew it was time for sleep and obediently lay down.

There was no crying. Not a peep out of him. *Ever.*

We were watching a movie when, for the first time, he walked into the living room after bedtime. As new parents, we were shocked— wondering how he had escaped his crib!

We repeated the bedtime routine, but this time we positioned ourselves near the door to watch him climbing over the top and down like a monkey!

Ever afterward, fearing injury, we left the side down. He could come and go as he pleased, free of the crib's bars from that night forward.

Life is like that. For months, seasons, years, we find ourselves enslaved. Perhaps a major life event caused the downward spiral or an unwise choice. Whatever the reason, the struggle to *break free* and *live carefree* is exhausting.

The truth is that the imagined jail cell has an open door. We can bolt at any time, with hope, help, and healing from the Savior. A tiny first step—a baby step toward Jesus—becomes a giant step toward freedom.

Only Jesus has the power to transform lives—for the weak, the weary, the discouraged. He says, "Come to Me, all who are weary and heavy-laden, and I will give you rest. Take My yoke upon you and learn from Me, for I am gentle and humble in heart, and you will find rest for your souls. For My yoke is easy and My burden is light." (Matthew 11:28–30)

You are invited. Come to Jesus and find rest.

The Giant Slayer

God's Protection, Care, and Deliverance

One of our granddaughter Annalee's favorite pastimes is watching the movie *Jack the Giant Slayer* with Granddaddy. A takeoff from the Jack and the Beanstalk story, a huge vine grows to the heavens, where giants live. Jack, a commoner, kills the giants and saves the king's daughter to live happily ever after.

Though Annie has memorized every imaginary scene with action rolling and danger imminent, she still becomes fearful. Her hiding place is behind Granddaddy!

We seem to never outgrow our fearful tendencies. Giants invade our imagination. We ponder bad things that could happen. It's a lesson in unreality.

The reality is that there is not one moment in time that the Lord is absent. He is constantly going before us to slay the giants—helping, strengthening, encouraging, and delivering us from now, until we arrive at the King's palace to live happily ever after!

"You are my hiding place; You preserve me from trouble; You surround me with songs of deliverance. Selah" (Psalm 32:7).

Where There's Smoke, There's Fire

God's Forgiveness and Invitation for Relationship with Him

Doing yard work is never ending at our home, no matter the season. Autumn especially is a busy time with piles and piles of leaves.

We have explored every avenue to deal with them, every piece of equipment—vacuum, blower, mower. You name it; we've tried it.

It hasn't always been that way. Our first leaf protocol was using the tried-and-true rake and wheelbarrow. Our first burn pile was the ditch at a very large tile that ran under Hiwassee Road, at the corner of our yard. The ditch was deep and wide, a perfect place to dump wheelbarrows of leaves.

An errand had sent my husband, Irad, to town. After much work, we were on a roll—the burn pile was full. Deciding to expedite the situation, I found a gas can with just enough gas to douse the leaf pile really *good*—and set it ablaze! The flames got out of control. Irad arrived home as my panic set in!

Taking immediate action, he picked up the nearest yard implement and began beating back the spreading flames—and sent me for the hose. I dragged it one hundred fifty feet to the flames, and I ran back to turn on the water. With the water, Irad began to get the fire under control. The smoke billowed out of both ends of the large road tile, forming an impenetrable cloud. Traffic was slow as the cars carefully navigated their way through the smoky cloud.

I left Irad standing by the road to guard the flames and to face the passersby with hose in hand. Regretting my foolishness, *I ran*—escaping into the house to hide.

Scripture teaches about fire and smoke—when God came down to earth. He had brought the children of Israel out of Egypt, into the wilderness, a deliverance from slavery with a promise of a new homeland.

"Now Mount Sinai was all in smoke because the Lord descended upon it in fire; and its smoke ascended like the smoke of a furnace, and the whole mountain quaked violently. When the sound of the trumpet grew louder and louder, Moses spoke and God answered him with thunder. The Lord came down on Mount Sinai, to the top of the mountain; and the Lord called Moses to the top of the mountain, and Moses went up" (Exodus 19:18–20).

Envision that! The one who created the universe came down to His chosen ones in fire and smoke!

What is our reaction today? We can try to escape Him, running and hiding, and miss His glory.

Or, like Moses, we can *go up* and experience the eternal flame of His love.

Which to choose?

Choose God. *Go up* to the Father. You will never regret it.

In the Blink of an Eye

God's Patience, Endurance, Love, and Future Plans

Life flies by. We anticipate a special day in the future—then in a flash it's gone. The same goes for loved ones. Tragedy strikes and regret fights for a place in our mind. We should have paid more attention ... done things differently. The list is long.

Oh, if we could simply erase the bad memories and keep the good.

It's interesting that the Father is able to remember our sins no more. "For I will forgive their wickedness and will remember their sins no more" (Hebrews 8:12 NIV).

It's puzzling how He does that. After all, we were made in His likeness. Should we not be able to *remember no more*?

Perhaps it has to do with the ability to forgive and to love selflessly. When forgiveness is born in our hearts, it must be nurtured by love of others more than self.

The world teaches a different message. We have heard or have spoken sayings such as "Stand up for yourself" or "Don't let them run over you".

Perhaps the spiritual gift of meekness would help.

"Blessed are the meek, for they will inherit the earth" (Matthew 5:5 NIV).

And it could be we are limited to eyesight that is worldly, not heavenly.

The Father knows that we are in the battle of our lives—for life eternal.

Even the angels marvel at His love and His forgiveness of our sinful nature.

"...When they spoke of the things that have now been told you by those who have preached the gospel to you by the Holy Spirit sent from heaven. Even angels long to look into these things ..." (1 Peter 1:12 NIV).

The plan is in place. "'For I know the plans I have for you,' declares the LORD, 'plans to prosper you and not to harm you, plans to give you hope and a future. Then you will call on me and come and pray to me, and I will listen to you.'" (Jeremiah 29:11–12 NIV).

And so His message is clear. Follow Him. Embrace each day we are given; our family and our little ones (even when they are not little any more). They are gifts from the Father.

Yes, we experience pain and regret in our earthly bodies. So did Jesus. He endured the pain, and His regret and yearning were for us.

"Jerusalem, Jerusalem, you who kill the prophets and stone those sent to you, how often I have longed to gather your children together, as a hen gathers her chicks under her wings, and you were not willing" (Luke 13:34 NIV).

He doesn't force. He simply waits for life to take its course. Then we come running to Him for all of our needs.

The Chain Gang

God's Victory for Belief and Warning for Unbelief

After almost a lifetime—years of working out of state, away from his family—Lindy, Irad's brother, came home.

At Lindy's homecoming, the family celebrated. Another celebration took place in heaven. Lindy joined the family of God—set free from judgment of sin.

> Truly I am your servant, LORD;
> I serve you just as my mother did;
> you have freed me from my chains.
> (Psalm 116:16 NIV)

Lindy was no longer in chains. Just maybe that's the reason he was drawn to men's prison ministry.

Scripture records stories of many prisoners. John the Baptist, a first cousin of Jesus. Peter. The apostle John. Paul. And other believers put in chains.

The greatest tragedy occurred when Jesus was taken.

"After arresting Him, he put Him in prison, handing him over to be guarded by four squads of four soldiers ... " (Acts 12:4 NIV).

There was another well-known prisoner.

"(Barabbas had been thrown into prison for an insurrection in the city, and for murder.)" (Luke 23:19 NIV).

Jesus was crucified and Barabbas set free. A prisoner swap—unjust in our eyes—yet a crystal-clear picture of redemption. For we are no different than Barabbas: sinful, fallen. " ... all our righteous acts are like filthy rags" (Isaiah 64:6 NIV).

Jesus solved our guilty verdict.

"Therefore, my friends, I want you to know that through Jesus the forgiveness of sins is proclaimed to you. Through Him everyone who believes is set free from every sin ... " (Acts 13:38–39 NIV).

Those who remain chained to sin are destined for wrath—a tragic end. But for those who believe, as did Lindy, there's a different ending.

"With God we will gain the victory, and he will trample down our enemies" (Psalm 60:12 NIV).

Come Out, Come Out, Wherever You Are

God's Response to Those Who Desire Relationship with Him

One of the great games of childhood was playing hide and seek. We scrambled for special hiding places. The game gained importance when adults played.

Our children and grandchildren love to play outside in the dark. They climb trees and lie on branches, hanging over the unsuspecting seeker—the one who is *It*.

Early on in our marriage, many years ago, we lived in a mobile home.

One of my favorite hide-and-seek memories dates back to when our firstborn, Irad III, was two years old.

Age didn't matter; we loved playing hide and seek with our baby boy. Irad III was always my partner. My husband, Irad, was *It*.

Indoors, there were few places to hide; creativity was required. Up until this occasion, the baby and I had lost the game every single time.

Determined to win, I noticed an empty laundry basket in the baby's bedroom. I set the basket on top of the chest of drawers, placed Irad III inside, instructing him to be very still, and quiet. I casually stood as a sentinel by the chest in the event of any movement by the baby.

Game on. I called for my husband to come and find the baby. There were only two places to look—the closet and under the bed. No baby.

Irad couldn't find him and thought that perhaps I had hidden him in another room.

We were the champs that day! The baby and I won for the first time.

I have wondered who invented hide and seek. I realized it must have begun with Adam and Eve. They were outside; and had just disobeyed the Father. Realizing they were naked, they hid. God was the seeker that time.

It's now up to us to seek Him. For the Lord says, "I love those who love Me, and those who diligently seek Me will find Me" (Proverbs 8:17).

Seek God. It's a game changer! We win!

Heaven Bound

God's Provision and Blessings for Seekers

It was one o'clock in the morning. Driving on an unfamiliar road miles from home, my husband, Irad, and I found ourselves in a predicament. The interstate was new; traffic was sparse; gas stations were nonexistent. We were anxious, tired, hungry, and very low on fuel. Poorly lit exits advertised gas, but stations had closed. We burned precious gas in searching.

We were driving on fumes when we saw it: a light on the horizon—an oasis. Closer, the light became bright. We found everything we needed: a gas fill up, the last motel room, and a Waffle House. Bacon and eggs had never tasted so good!

Similar is the journey of a believer in the Lord Jesus.

The road is not frequented by crowds and is sometimes dark. At times we are fearful, weary, simply "out of gas".

Ever been there?

The Word of God shows us the way to vitality. The search is worth the effort—not a search for gas but a search for the light, the assurance in God's Word that there's a rest stop up ahead.

"The unfolding of your word gives light; it gives understanding to the simple" (Psalm 119:130 NIV).

One way to fuel up is to learn humility.

"Humble yourselves in the presence of the Lord, and He will exalt you" (James 4:10).

Sometimes when traveling, we stop for directions. Along the road, fellow believers point to help, provide food for thought. "*Like* apples of gold in settings of silver is a word spoken in right circumstances" (Proverbs 25:11).

"And I heard a voice from heaven, saying, 'Write, "Blessed are the dead who die in the Lord from now on!"' 'Yes,' says the Spirit, 'they will rest from their labor, for their deeds will follow with them'" (Revelation 14:13 NIV).

Confessions from the Heart

God's Promise of Forgiveness upon Confession and Repentance

Some of the scariest places are on rides at the county fair. When our children were small, anticipation sparkled in their eyes when going to the fair was mentioned. Upon arrival at the fair, my panic would begin. I was fearful of high rides. Nobody wanted to be joined by a party pooper; so, with the bravest smile I could muster, I embraced the adventure.

Irad would buy tickets for *all* the rides. We began with the Tilt–a–Whirl and merry–go–round. Those were rides on the ground; so far so good.

We advanced to faster rides. Irad and the kids would smile and tell me I could make it. The Mad Mouse roller coaster was high but fast, producing an adrenaline rush with no time to think. My family loved it.

Irad invited me to one last ride, the dreaded Ferris wheel. He assured me it would be fun—and that he would keep me safe. I relented and got on. The wheel moved slowly. Upon arrival at the top, our chair began to swing, slowly at first, and then faster. When I realized that Irad was rocking the chair, I screamed—then cried out to God for mercy.

Scripture teaches, "Whoever conceals their sins does not prosper, but the one who confesses and renounces them finds mercy" (Proverbs 28:13 NIV).

I shouted confessions from the top my lungs aloft that Ferris wheel!

The entire county must have heard my prayer that night. Irad tried to quiet me, to no avail. The prayer ended when my feet hit the pavement! The Lord delivered me.

Many years have passed and I still give the Lord a *shout out* at a threat, whether perceived or real. The Lord is faithful. Irad has retained his sense of humor and he keeps me safe! We've experienced many adventures together, but never, ever again on a Ferris wheel.

Praise God from whom all blessings flow!

How Does Your Garden Grow?

God's Instruction for Answered Prayer

In years past, Irad and I have planted vegetable gardens. Going overboard and buying too many plants and too much seed, I'm usually in a frenzy to get started.

Working up the soil is crucial, as is laying out the garden with lines absolutely straight.

Radishes and onions are sown in the front row with a space for spinach and lettuce.

The cherished tomato plants are planted next.

Last to be sown are beans, cucumbers, squash, peppers. The corn stands tall on the back row.

The plants of the garden are like people—many different kinds and flavors. God made us that way.

The garden begins to flourish; the battle begins in earnest against weeds, rabbits, groundhogs, and bad weather.

Spiritual life is like that. The seed of the Word is sown. New life is born.

Then the worries of life begin—weeds choking out the good. Sin is like a weed in the garden; we must yank it out before it overruns and smothers the fruit. And bear fruit we must, for answered prayer. For the Lord says,

> You did not choose me, but I chose you and appointed you so that you might go and bear fruit—fruit that will last—and so that whatever you ask in my name the Father will give you. (John 15:16 NIV)

God's Waiting Room

God's Exaltation for Those Who Are Humble

Without exception, everyone has waited for something. We've waited at hospitals for news, at front doors for family members, at restaurants for food. The list is endless.

One of the most frustrating waits is on a phone call when we are placed on hold. We hear an automated voice: "One moment please" or "Your call is important to us." Then silence. We check to see if the call is still active. Minutes tick by.

Prayer can be like that—waiting in silence for God to "pick up".

His hold button must still be flashing.

Perhaps motives are the reason.

"When you ask, you do not receive, because you ask with wrong motives, that you may spend what you get on your pleasures" (James 4:3 NIV).

Sound like the Lord's discipline?

It is.

But here's the cure. "Come near to God and he will come near to you. Wash your hands, you sinners, and purify your hearts, you double-minded…. Humble yourselves before the Lord, and he will lift you up." (James 4:8, 10 NIV).

God's Counsel, Intercession, Faithfulness, and Answers to Prayer

It was cool spring day, April 3, 1955. My twin sister, Dean, and I were at home on the farm. It was our fifth birthday.

Mama and Daddy were down at the chicken house preparing for the delivery of thirty thousand baby chicks. Fresh shavings were spread and coal-burning stoves were lit. No one noticed the hot coal roll out onto the shavings.

Everything was ready for the chicks, when the fire ignited. The blaze spread fast throughout the chicken house. The flames climbed higher and higher until they reached the storage shelves that held a large supply of dynamite.

Realizing the danger, everyone ran from the blaze. Mama and Daddy were standing on the hillside when the dynamite blew. Their eardrums were ruptured and bleeding from the blast. Water pipes broke at home, flooding the entire house. The explosion was felt a mile away and created a vast debris field. Mama said it blew that chicken house "from here to kingdom come"!

With the Lord's help, we survived the physical and financial devastation.

Many years later, the family faced devastation of a different sort. We needed our heavy burden lifted. It was imperative that I get in touch with the Lord and His power.

I sought Him through His Word and discovered a word for power in Ephesians 3:20: "Now to Him who is able to do far more abundantly beyond all that we ask or think, according to the power that works within us,". The Greek word for power in the verse is *dynamo*: the origin for the word—dynamite!

I knew dynamite! Dynamite is powerful, but according to my childhood experience, it was harmless when stored on a shelf. Dynamite required a flame to ignite its force.

I needed a match.

The Lord knew my heart was searching. He revealed to me a message that deepened my relationship to the Father. Written in James 5:16, it stated, "…The effective fervent prayer of a righteous man avails much" (NKJV).

To make sure I understood the verse, I looked up each word in the Greek dictionary. "Effective"—*energeó*: to be at work. "Fervent"—*zeó*: to boil, be hot. "Availeth"—*ischuó*: to be strong, have power.

I had found the match!

My prayer changed that night. "Oh Lord, help me pray *dynamite* prayers—the kind that blast through the heavens straight to the throne of God."

Years have passed since that night. I cannot explain how the Holy Spirit translates my heart's desire into words understood in heaven.

But this I know with certainty: "Before they call, I will answer; while they are still speaking I will hear" (Isaiah 65:24 NIV).

As Easy as A, B, C

God's Attention to the Prayers of Believers

Saturdays were fun days when I was growing up in the '50s. Mama would make scratch meals through the week, but Saturdays were different. We went to the grocery store and were treated to some of our favorite ready-to-eat foods. Campbell's tomato soup was my sister Dean's choice. Mine was alphabet soup.

I loved the novelty of having ABCs in my vegetable soup. Yet the taste of Mama's homemade vegetable soup was unrivaled!

Homemade vegetable soup is easy breezy to make. Toss in many different ingredients—leftovers in the refrigerator, contents of cans from the cabinets—season it with salt, and let it simmer.

Permeating the whole house, the aroma is wonderful and remarkably comforting! It's curious that we don't make homemade soup more often.

The Father has similar experiences when we pray. There is a large golden censer in God's living room (the throne room). It's kept hot as it sits on the golden altar.

Our prayers to the Father, all different and varied, go into the golden censer. An angel adds seasoning: incense ("and the smoke of the incense, with the prayers of the saints, went up before God…" (Revelation 8:4).

Just as with making easy-breezy homemade soup, it's curious that we don't offer more prayers.

Stand by Me

God's Encouragement and Faithfulness in Answering Prayer

Agony. Of all the words in the English language, it is one of the most dreaded.

Experienced in different forms such as physical pain, rejection, or mental anguish, agony begins with pain deep within. I once read it portrayed as "the dark night of the soul", and apt description.

Pouring out one's heart before the Lord transcends space and time, into heaven … straight to the throne of God. It matters not the reason—only the Lord's faithfulness.

His answers come in different ways, and they never fail to reassure and delight.

As I prevailed upon the Lord one evening, my prayer was long and disjointed. It was in the wee hours of a Sunday morning—church day.

We awakened late but made it to church. With my phone off, as I worshipped, singing praises to His name, my inner pain lessened a bit.

As I left church—phone reactivated—a text message pinged from an unfamiliar number received at 11:00 a.m. It read, "Just wanted to let you know that you are appreciated for your love towards God—and that he sees your every need."

It was as if the text dropped right out of heaven! It took my breath away. I entitled it "Word from the Lord, October, 2013." I saved the message and read it many times in weeks to come. It reassured me once again that Jesus is trustworthy.

It was a few months later that I accidentally discovered the sender. A business contact and faithful servant of the Lord, working out of state many miles away, not knowing a thing about my family's circumstances, had been impressed to send me the message dictated by God that Sunday morning. The Lord Jesus came to my rescue—*again*.

Praise His name.

"And I saw heaven opened, and behold, a white horse, and He who sat on it *is* called Faithful and True … " (Revelation 19:11).

There's More Than Meets the Eye

God's Strength and Protection

In the 1970s, our family watched a TV favorite, *The Six Million Dollar Man*. The TV series portrayed a former astronaut with bionic implants in his legs, arm, and eye.

The result was extraordinary speed, strength, and vision. He did amazing things with his bionic eye—zoom—seeing at night, detecting heat. His vision helped him beat the bad guys every week!

The Lord designed our eyes to see in the physical realm, but there is another—the spiritual realm—just as real. Angels exist there as God's messengers, as lifeguards for His children, and as warriors against evil.

Elisha prayed and his servant saw the angels. The army of the Lord encircled around them, with horses and flaming chariots, in protection from evil King Aram (see 2 Kings 6:8–23).

To obtain spiritual eyesight, no bionic eye is required—only trust and prayer. Otherwise, one surrenders peace on the altar of fear.

When peril approaches, remember Elisha's words: "'Don't be afraid,' the prophet answered. 'Those who are with us are more than those who are with them'" (2 Kings 6:16 NIV).

Everything's Coming Up Roses

God's Love, Faithfulness, Comfort, Peace, and Care for His Children

For years, she dreamed of planting a red rambling rose bush to climb on the awning of the front porch of her house. She finally planted one in the fall of 1973.

My mama, Katherine Elizabeth Howard, loved rearing her girls—five daughters.

Mama was killed instantly in a car crash on February 18, 1974. I was twenty-three and not ready for her to depart for heaven.

For months prior to her death, fearing a lingering illness, she would snap her fingers and say she wanted to go "just like that"—instantly.

Mama had visited with her siblings the week of her accident. A spontaneous decision, she had taken a rare day away from the farm and had driven to Dayton, Tennessee, her hometown. She spent time with her sisters and brother. She said she had a wonderful day!

The day following her accident, our phone rang. A lady who worked in a clothing store in our town gave us her condolences and conveyed a message. Mama had shopped her store earlier in the week and had confided joyfully that her children were raised—married to good men—and that she was ready to leave for heaven.

During Mama's funeral, an unexpected emotion overcame me. Not sadness—no tear escaped my eyes. The feeling was intense: calmness, peace, joy.

Then, forlorn about my reaction, I felt shame. Had I not loved her enough to cry?

Afterward, all of my sisters described experiencing the same emotions.

I wasn't alone.

With the funeral over, my sisters stayed to help sort Mama's personal items. Four days later, my oldest sister, Nancy, left to fly home to West Tennessee. On the airplane, Nancy began small talk with a woman seated next to her, a stranger. Nancy asked what she did for a living. The woman responded by saying she was involved with a national prayer chain. In turn, the woman asked Nancy why she was traveling. Nancy revealed she was returning from Madisonville.

The stranger, looking surprised, said her prayer chain had been praying for the family of a woman from Madisonville who had been killed in a car crash. She asked if Nancy had known her.

The name? Katherine Elizabeth Howard.

Three months later in May 1974, Mother's Day arrived—the first one without Mama.

Driving past our childhood home, I saw it: Mama's rambling rose bush, covered for the first time in stunning red roses.

"Precious in the sight of the LORD is the death of his faithful servants" (Psalm 116:15 NIV).

What Becomes of the Brokenhearted?

God's Gentleness, Compassion, Healing, and Deliverance for His Children

A broken heart is caused by life experiences—of every nature. The wounded heart, in its tenderness, is where the Lord does His finest work, before the scarring and hardening can take hold.

"He heals the brokenhearted and binds up their wounds" (Psalm 147:3).

Many are the experiences of life. Jesus our Lord called this tribulation. Anything that we endure He endured more; any emotions that we feel, He felt even greater—sorrow, betrayal, pain …

He says, "Come to Me all who labor and are heavy burdened and I will give you rest."

Our part is to come and be tenderly cared for by Jesus.

"You have taken account of my wanderings; put my tears in your bottle. Are *they* not recorded in your book?" (Psalm 56:8).

Sentimental Journey

God's Love, Gentleness, and Attention to Actions of His Children

I so admire people who do scrapbooks—those creative and talent-rich books with every page marked with special memorabilia! It's an act of love.

My pictures are crammed haphazardly into three drawers—cherished memories run amok.

One day our daughter, Julia, asked me to search for a particular picture. My heart sank. Searching took a long time, not only due to organizational chaos. Each picture took me back on a sentimental journey.

Finding the requested photo was a monumental task of gigantic proportions!

Pictures stored in the cloud are the answer for my dilemma! And they are definitely stored there. Not in the Internet cloud, but in the cloud in the Third Heaven where God lives.

For the Father keeps a memory book, and He records important moments. Not the occasions we believe to be important, but those *He* does.

"Then those who feared the Lord spoke to one another, and the Lord gave attention and heard *it*, and a book of remembrance was written before Him for those who fear the Lord and who esteem His name" (Malachi 3:16).

A book of remembrance—imagine that!

I wonder how many times the Heavenly Father looks at it?

Maybe in moments when He's feeling sentimental.

His act of love.

Tears on My Pillow

God's Comfort, Strength, Victory, and Answered Prayer for His Children

It was 1958 when "Tears on My Pillow" was released by Little Anthony and the Imperials. It became their signature song. And it has been rerecorded through the years by various artists—a Golden Oldie gone viral!

Everyone has experienced it: tears on pillows, pain in hearts. What to do when the pain of loss becomes unbearable? It was July 2, 1997, when our daughter-in-law, Angelia departed for heaven, leaving our son and grandson—her young husband and one-year-old firstborn son. The Lee/Crawley family was devastated.

For days on end, setting personal pain aside, comforting loved ones, and being carried on the wings of the Father's grace, I thought I was too strong to crumble.

Very late one night, with a groaning deep within, I remained awake. Sleep escaped me. The emotional pain was unbearable; I knew not how to pray and cried to the Father these words: "Lord, please wake someone up to pray for us."

It took about half an hour to experience relief. At two o'clock in the morning, physically and emotionally exhausted, I was finally able to find sweet rest.

Three days later, when I was off from work, driving to town, I noticed our water bill in my purse. Odd. I always paid the bill at the bank when it arrived in the mail (never at City Hall). I had forgotten to pay it and it was due that day. I was one block from City Hall. After circling City Hall twice, unfamiliar with the drive-through lane, I eventually located the narrow alley and stopped at the drive-through window.

There, I was greeted by a city employee and friend. I did not know it at the time, but she was just filling in at the drive-through; her regular job assignment was in another part of the building. Most everyone in town knew of Angelia's leaving; she was no exception. She asked how we were doing.

With inexpressible grief, I answered, "Oh, pretty good."

Her next statement was a bombshell. She said, "You know, three nights ago I was dead asleep in my bed. I woke up and couldn't go back to sleep until I prayed for y'all."

So overcome with unspeakable joy for the Lord's faithfulness, I could not convey to her the significance of her statement. I hope that I thanked her for her obedience. I simply do not remember.

What I do remember is that my heart was filled with praise to overflowing as I departed and turned onto the street.

Many years have passed. Our family has walked through much heartache since. Living on this side of heaven, tears of sorrow abound.

Others may not have experienced what is expressed by the words of Psalm 20:6–8, but I can attest to it with absolute assurance.

Now I know that the LORD saves His anointed; He will answer him from His holy heaven, with the saving strength of His right hand. Some *boast* in chariots and some in horses, but we will boast in the name of the LORD, our God. They have bowed down and fallen, but we have risen and stood upright.

Praise His name!

Picking Up the Pieces

God's Compassion and Healing for His Children

The year 1968 was a time of "firsts" for my husband, Irad, and me.

A first residence (a twelve-by-sixty-two-foot mobile home), lacking style points, but we were happy. Then, our first Christmas together as a married couple.

Those were the days when blue Christmas lights were in vogue and mega department stores made their appearance in East Tennessee. We purchased decorations for the tree at the Almart on Clinton Highway in Knoxville, Tennessee. The store seemed huge by local standards. We found beautiful blue glass ornaments in many shapes—balls, icicles, and bells.

By Christmas of 2013, forty-five years later, all of the ornaments had been broken except a solitary blue bell. Though its luster had long since faded, our grandchildren loved seeing this fragile ornament on the tree.

We didn't anticipate the tree falling over. The 1968 blue bell ornament lay shattered on the floor.

That's what happens in life. Things appear to be normal, and disaster strikes. Lives are shattered.

Job would understand. "I was at ease, but He shattered me, And He has grasped me by the neck and shaken me to pieces; He has also set me up as His target" (Job 16:12).

Having been faithful to God, Job knew God had allowed the devastating events into Job's life. Disheartened, sick, and grieving, Job sought the Lord in humility. The Lord delivered Job from brokenness, restoring his possessions and social standing; the Lord also blessed Job with more sons and daughters.

Though Job's life was different, "The Lord blessed the latter days of Job more than his beginning" (Job 42:12).

The Lord desires to heal brokenness.

Our shattered first Christmas ornament looks different these days. We picked up the pieces, put them in a clear ornament, and hung them on our 2014 Christmas tree. The ornament represents a new first for our family. It's a symbol to remind us of the Father's abiding grace and compassion, for He heals shattered lives.

"But for you who revere my name, the sun of righteousness will rise with healing in its rays. And you will go out and frolic like well-fed calves" (Malachi 4:2 NIV).

Mind Games

God's Wisdom, Counsel, and Care for His Children

Some might remember the days of eight-track tapes. They hit our market in East Tennessee in the early 1960s. We enjoyed our first experience with eight tracks in our sister Linda's car, a 1964- ½ Mustang convertible. What a car!

My twin, Dean, and I were sixteen when Linda bought the car. She was so generous, allowing us to drive her car whenever we wanted.

The next audio technology development was cassette tapes. We equally loved cassette tapes. Using the tape player's rewind and replay button, we could play the same favorite song over and over.

The human psyche is equipped with a rewind/replay button too.

We make mistakes. The mind's rewind/replay button activates. In the battlefield of the mind, past actions are remembered again and again, producing regret, guilt, and shame.

The ultimate results? Self-punishment. Mental enslavement. Anguish.

Forgiveness of self is denied.

And yet reliving past failures is contrary to the Lord.

"Forget the former things; do not dwell on the past. See, I am doing a new thing! Now it springs up; do you not perceive it…?" (Isaiah 43:18–19 NIV).

"No temptation has overtaken you except such as is common to man, but God *is* faithful …" (1 Corinthians 10:13 NKJV).

The Lord bore our shame and guilt.

"*There is* therefore now no condemnation for those who are in Christ Jesus" (Romans 8:1 NKJV).

He set us free.

"It was for freedom that Christ set us free; therefore keep standing firm and do not be subject again to a yoke of slavery" (Galatians 5:1).

The Lord has forgiven us.

> I acknowledged my sin to You,
> And my iniquity I have not hidden.
> I said, "I will confess my transgressions to the Lord,"
> And You forgave the iniquity of my sin. Selah.
> (Psalm 32:5 NKJV)

He heals us with His Word.

"Finally, brothers and sisters, whatever is true, whatever is noble, whatever is right, whatever is pure, whatever is lovely, whatever is admirable—if anything is excellent or praiseworthy—think about such things" (Philippians 4:8 NIV).

The battlefield of the mind belongs to the Lord.

The Storm

God's Life Lessons, Power, Deliverance, and Miracles

It was April 1965. I was at home with Daddy and my twin sister, Dean. Mama had traveled to North Carolina to assist our older sister, Pat, with her firstborn, Steve.

Our three chicken houses, each three hundred feet long, were full—eighty thousand broiler chickens almost ready for market. At night, lights were turned out so the chickens could roost.

The weather forecast that evening was warm with thunderstorms and a tornado watch. Thunderstorms are the worst kind of forecast in an East Tennessee spring.

Dean and I were asleep when Daddy awakened us. He needed us. The thunderous storm had arrived. Unless we intervened, the chickens would pile up onto each other and smother.

Each of us went to a chicken house. Dean was in the lower house and Daddy the middle. I was in the upper house. Our assignment was to "walk out" each house, scattering the chickens.

With fierce winds and lightning strikes all around them, the chickens were piling up, warm and wet. I walked alone in the darkness—only able to see when the night sky lit up. At the end of my house were two huge doors. Typically they opened by turning inward, but the wind had whipped them outward—opposite the hinges. The chickens were flying out in droves. I attempted to right the doors, but I was not strong enough.

I was desperate for help to save my chickens. With the lashing rain on my face mingling with tears, I ran barefoot down the gravel lane between the upper and middle house, screaming for Daddy's help. The howling wind carried my cries away. Thunder shook the ground.

It was a miracle he heard me and that he found Dean in the lower house. We ran together to the upper house. It was useless to try to shout to each other over the fury of the storm. We knew what we must do. The three of us pushed with every ounce of strength, repositioning the doors.

Years later, I asked Daddy how many chickens we lost that night. He said that he thought, "We did alright… that the storm didn't *sink us*"!

The Lord's disciples experienced a violent storm.

> But as they sailed he fell asleep: and there came down a storm of wind on the lake; and they were filling with water, and were in jeopardy.
>
> And they came to him, and awoke him, saying, Master, master, we perish. And he awoke, and rebuked the wind and the raging of the water: and they ceased, and there was a calm.
>
> And he said unto them, Where is your faith? And being afraid they marveled, saying one to another, Who then is this, that he commandeth even the winds and the water, and they obey him. (Luke 8:23–25 ASV)

The Lord was with his disciples. They too stayed afloat!

More Than Skin Deep

God's Love and Deliverance in Response to
Prayer, Perseverance, and Courage

Most everyone can name someone who everyone wants to be around!
We have one of those *someones* in our family.

Of the five girls born to Mama and Daddy, Linda was the adorable
middle child! Endowed with beauty and charm, gifted to be the ultimate
hostess, she makes living life look easy.

Her secret essence is humility, selflessness, and love. Quietly caring
for her family and making provision for others, she takes care of the
important things in life. Linda's beauty is more than skin deep.

So it was with Queen Esther. Scripture records her unparalleled beauty.
"Esther found favor in the eyes of all who saw her" (Esther 2:15).

King Ahasuerus chose her as his queen. He soon discovered that her
beauty was more than skin deep too.

Queen Esther, a Jew, was selfless and humble. She placed her own life
in jeopardy to save her kindred and to foil an evil plot to destroy her
people, devised by a Persian named Haman.

Esther said, "Go, gather together all the Jews who are in Susa, and
fast for me. Do not eat or drink for three days, night or day. I and my

attendants will fast as you do. When this is done, I will go to the king, even though it is against the law. And if I perish, I perish" (Esther 4:16 NIV).

Esther hosted a banquet for the king, revealed Haman's evil plot to the king over dinner, and saved her people (Esther 5–8).

Because of the depth of Queen Esther's love, God's chosen people were saved.

God is love and has a plan to save His people through faith in Jesus. God's love never fails.

"neither height nor depth, nor anything else in all creation, will be able to separate us from the love of God that is in Christ Jesus our Lord" (Romans 8:39 NIV).

What Time Is It?

God's Fulfilled Prophecy and His Compassion for the Children of Israel

Once perfected by days of practice, whistling is becoming a lost art. Do guys whistle at girls anymore? Fun but perhaps considered politically incorrect!

My husband, Irad, is the World's Whistle King! His whistle can be heard for a mile. He trained our children and grandchildren to come running at his distinct whistle. His whistled messages signaled, "It's time to go."

The Heavenly Father whistles too! It's His way of fulfilling prophecy.

It is written in the Bible that Israel's disobedience and evil lifestyle caused the Lord to disperse them from their homeland and settle them over the whole world. The Father promised that "in the last days", He would call them home and restore them and their beloved land.

"I will whistle for them and gather them together; For I have redeemed them; and they will be as numerous as before" (Zechariah 10:8).

On May 14, 1948, a red-letter day on God's calendar, the State of Israel was reborn before the nations of the world. More than six million Jews have been re-gathered to their homeland.

"He will raise a banner for the nations and gather the exiles of Israel; he will assemble the scattered people of Judah from the four quarters of the earth" (Isaiah 11:12 NIV).

"You will arise and have compassion on Zion, for it is time to show favor to her; the appointed time has come" (Psalm 102:13 NIV).

Have you checked the time?

The Dead Ringer

God's Wake-Up Warning to the Church

Heralding each new day, roosters have been sounding the wake-up call for centuries—country living at its best!

There is, however, a time and place for everything.

Daddy acquired macular degeneration and congestive heart failure in his seventies. At age eighty-four, he was still farming, and our goal was to maintain his mobility.

His physician advised us to keep check on fluid retention, so we purchased scales that told him what he weighed. A cell phone helped him communicate on the farm. Another device, his digital pocket clock, spoke the time at the press of a button. The clock also had an alarm; though not needed, a cock-a-doodle-doo sound was set for the mornings.

Carried every day for months, the rooster clock began to crow at odd times throughout the day. Daddy couldn't hear it. With the operating directions long since lost, we couldn't seem to fix it.

It was a Sunday morning when Irad and I stopped to help Daddy dress for church. We arrived and sat in the fifth row. When the sermon was about to begin, Daddy quietly pulled out his clock to check the time.

Irad and I exchanged looks, both remembering with alarm that the rooster could crow at any time.

Just the thought of it crowing in church ...

Scripture records a famous rooster: the one that crowed when Peter denied Jesus (Mark 14:72).

And no—Daddy's rooster clock did not crow. The ringer must have died.

I'm glad for him that it did not sound the alarm, but perhaps its crowing might have awakened the church.

"*Do* this, knowing the time, that it is already the hour for you to awaken from sleep; for now salvation is nearer to us than when we believed" (Romans 13:11).

A Half Truth Is a Whole Lie

God's Reaction to Disobedience

Election Day in rural America was a thing to behold in the 1950s. In preparation for the big day, a flatbed trailer was parked in front of the Monroe County Court House with a line of huge chalkboards set up on its floor. All of the county's thirteen precincts were listed.

As a nine-year-old, I could recite the name of every precinct. Daddy loved politics—and so did I!

So much has changed since the days of paper ballots and open and honest discourse. In the politics of modern culture, there seems to be a growing sense of censorship about speaking truth.

For those who dare to speak out, the earthly penalty is great. The lone voice is rejected—drowned out by many. The Word teaches that men in society will be "holding to a form of godliness, although they have denied its power; Avoid such men as these" (2 Timothy 3:5).

Jesus did not agree with the rulers of His day. He knew that the authorities were making laws that caused the people to suffer.

Jesus was rejected by His community, despised by the religious leaders of His synagogue and betrayed by His friends.

"From this time many of his disciples turned back and no longer followed him" (John 6:66 NIV).

A life lived with virtue is a choice and is guided from above. Speaking truth is paramount for pleasing the Lord; for He hates a liar (see Proverbs 6:16–19).

America's founding fathers spoke out against injustices by those in authority, and a nation was born.

Censorship is a danger to our way of life on earth, and ultimately, life eternal.

God is allowing America to serve itself, not Him. Our leaders in their political correctness have abandoned Christian values. Jesus experienced the same.

Jesus openly called King Herod a fox (Luke 13:31-33).

Americans seem to have become as the Pharisees of Jesus' day—claiming the Church but lacking His power.

Jesus turned the "Pharisee operated Synagogue" upside down; saying to them, 'My House shall be called a House of Prayer'; but you are making it a Robbers' Den.' (Matthew 21:12–13)

He will do the same for our communities—our country. Pray for communities across America to return to the Lord.

Pray for the silent majority to be silent no longer.

The Lord instructs us: what we should do and what we should say in times like these.

> "These are the things which you should do: speak the truth to one another; judge with truth and judgment for peace in your gates. Also let none of you devise evil in your heart against another, and do not love perjury; for all these are what I hate,' declares the LORD." (Zechariah 8:16–17)

Just between You, Me, and the Fencepost

God's Love, Healing, Comfort, Care, and Deliverance for His Children

Georgie Tate Lee, my mother-in-law, was precious to me. I called her Nanaw. A study in contrasts, she was gentle as a lamb, but was courageous as a lion; refined as any lady, but worked like a Trojan; loved diamonds, but was a pro with her mattock. She didn't drive, but she could tell you how!

It was my pleasure to be her companion, friend, and helper. On one particular occasion, she called. She needed help. The day had dawned when she could wait no longer. The ugly barbed-wire fence behind her house had to go!

Upon arrival, I discovered she had removed the entire fence except for one last post. With the sun blazing, we pushed, pulled, and lifted, over and over—until that stubborn, gnarly post came out! Though dirty and sweaty, we were jubilant!

There are seasons when our lives are exemplified by the barbed-wire fence and ugly post. The emotional response to painful life situations, at times, is not a pretty picture.

The Bible describes it as sin.

Attempting to go it alone and solve our own sin problem, we become shredded by the barbed wire of regret.

Help is essential to remove poisonous pillars of deeply seated resentments, unforgiving hearts, and insecurities resulting from old wounds, grief, and sorrows.

Desperate, we call for help. The Lord is pleased. He died to heal.

Isaiah 53:4 (KJV) says, "Surely he hath borne our griefs, and carried our sorrows: yet we did esteem him stricken, smitten of God, and afflicted."

Bathed in His love, we obtain victory by the work of the Holy Spirit.

"The Spirit of the Lord is upon me, because he hath anointed me to preach the gospel to the poor; he hath sent me to heal the brokenhearted, to preach deliverance to the captives, and recovering of sight to the blind, to set at liberty them that are bruised" (Luke 4:18 KJV).

Pushing the Panic Button

God's Response to the Faith of His Children

It's a mother's worst nightmare: her baby in danger. My twin sister Dean's firstborn, Ashley, was about a year old. Ashley was a beautiful baby. A pro at hiding objects in her mouth, she was terrifying to tend!

Finding Ashley taking a drink of cleaning fluid sent Dean into a panic of epic proportions. She grabbed the baby and the cleaning fluid bottle, with instructions ("Consult doctor if ingested").

The call to the doc was no help. An examination was needed. No time to waste. At the speed of light, Dean, baby, and cleaning fluid bottle arrived at the doctor's office. No front-desk check-in—Dean blazed through every exam room door until she found the doctor.

Holy Scripture records a similar story about a woman with her child in danger.

Jesus was in the vicinity of Tyre; He entered a house and did not want anyone to know it. He was having a meal when an unexpected visitor arrived. The mother's need was urgent. Her little girl had a demon. She had heard that Jesus was visiting her town. She believed in Jesus' power. She searched until she found Jesus, interrupted His visit, fell at His feet, and begged for her daughter's healing. (see Mark 7:24–29 and Matthew 15:21-28).

"Then Jesus said to her, 'Woman, you have great faith! Your request is granted.' And her daughter was healed at that moment" (Matthew 15:28 NIV).

She *heard, believed, took action.* We should do the same,

> looking unto Jesus, the author and finisher of *our* faith, who for the joy that was set before Him endured the cross, despising the shame, and has sat down at the right hand of the throne of God. (Hebrews 12:2 NKJV)

God's Rewards and Blessings for Obedience

I had the immense joy of sharing my childhood with my twin sister, Dean. We did everything together.

Our older sister, Pat, selected us for a twin behavior experiment in her child psychology class at the University of Tennessee in Knoxville.

With Mama's permission, Pat drove us to the UTK campus.

Our assignment was to play with other nine-year-old twins. Mama told Dean and me to behave as Pat and others observed us behind the glass wall.

A small prize was given to each participant. Pat reported angelic behavior.

We made Mama proud!

It's curious that best behavior is reserved for moments with acquaintances and strangers.

Our "A game" seems to disintegrate when we are around those we love the most—family and friends. Words and actions at home are not for public critique.

The Lord watches and gives rewards for good behavior.

> Do not repay evil with evil or insult with insult. On the contrary, repay evil with blessing, because to this you were called so that you may inherit a blessing. For "Whoever would love life and see good days must keep their tongue from evil and their lips from deceitful speech.
>
> They must turn from evil and do good; they must seek peace and pursue it.
>
> For the eyes of the Lord are on the righteous and his ears are attentive to their prayer, but the face of the Lord is against those who do evil." (1 Peter 3:9–12 NIV)

My Feet Don't Stink

God's Plan for Redeemed Family Members

On rare occasions, Daddy made an overnight business trip. He liked to look nice, but he relied on Mama to "put him together". She hung his suit and shirt in a suit bag, looped a tie over the hanger, and put a change of socks into a jacket pocket. He was set to go.

Many years later, I prepared Daddy for a road trip. He was showered, dressed and was leaving when I remembered his extra socks. Daddy waved me off, saying he didn't need a clean pair of socks—his feet didn't stink!

The Lord has something to say about dirty feet.

At the Last Supper, Jesus performed an act that only a beloved friend would do. He washed His disciples' feet. Eleven were all His, washed clean of sin. Their new life in Him had begun.

Just as the disciples were washed clean forever, so are we believers washed clean forever.

Along life's journey, our feet get dirty with unwise choices that lead to sin. Our walk with the Lord is disrupted.

All is not lost. Confess to the Lord. He will wash those dirty feet!

> Jesus *said to him, "He who has bathed needs only to wash
> his feet, but is completely clean; "(John 13:10)

Love That SS Chevelle

God's Rewards for Generosity

A prized possession is typically not loaned to anyone, let alone to two eloping teenagers. Though we secretly planned to get married, Irad and I had made no other arrangements.

Janie, Irad's sister, "found us out". She and her daughter, Rebecca Lee Kirkpatrick, began to make plans.

Rebecca's *fav* car of all time, her red 1964 SS Chevy Chevelle convertible, provided Irad and me transportation. Added to that was a full tank of gas, wedding bands, and Janie's twenty-dollar bill. To us, that was big money in 1968.

We didn't have to worry about the "something borrowed" tradition.

It *all* was. We owned nothing.

Generosity was Janie's trademark. And Rebecca learned from her mama. Like two peas in a pod, they gave us all we needed to tie the knot.

No warnings about not wrecking the car. No admonition for repayment.

They gave us big hugs and cheerful well wishes.

That was many years ago.

Living a verse out of the Bible came naturally for Janie and Rebecca.

"Command them to do good, to be rich in good deeds, and to be generous and willing to share. In this way they will lay up treasure for themselves as a firm foundation for the coming age, so that they may take hold of the life that is truly life" (1 Timothy 6:18–19 NIV).

Janie is enjoying her treasure in heaven—having already taken hold of the life which is truly life.

Rebecca, a lady in waiting, has her treasure stored up as a firm foundation for the coming age.

What do generous hearts look like?

The answer is a red 1964 SS Chevelle convertible, a full tank of gas, and a twenty-dollar bill.

Hanging by a String

God's Faithfulness for His Trusting Children

In 1981, the country was in a great recession, although in our household it was a time of great depression.

Our county's unemployment was at 25 percent, and home-mortgage interest rates were at 18 percent.

My husband, Irad, was a custom builder. No one was buying or building. Foreclosures were at an all-time high. The 25 percent of people with no job were hoping to hang on to what they had. The 75 percent who had jobs couldn't afford new house payments.

One could say Irad was in the 25 percent. He had a skill—and no building site to work on.

Our daughter, Julia, was ten and needed new school shoes. No, she hadn't outgrown them. Her shoes were just falling apart!

We had no money for new shoes—just spare change, enough to buy new shoelaces. Irad glued Julia's shoes, added new laces, and applied white shoe polish. The shoes looked like new when he was done. The repairs lasted one day!

What to do about shoes tomorrow?

The Lord teaches not to worry about food and clothes—nor about tomorrow.

"Therefore do not worry about tomorrow, for tomorrow will worry about itself. Each day has enough trouble of its own" (Matthew 6:34 NIV).

The Lord taught us many lessons during those times. To believe Him. To walk in faith. We continue to walk in faith—not knowing what tomorrow will bring, at times hanging on by our shoelaces.

Blessed assurance, Jesus is mine!

No Bull

God's Instruction and Wisdom for Life Situations

Daddy became ill suddenly in February 1998. I took him straight from the farm to the hospital. He never returned to his beloved farm.

Farm responsibilities did not stop with Daddy's leaving. The management and work were left to his family—five daughters and five sons-in-law— and our dairyman.

Operating the farm was complicated. There was a two-hundred-head dairy herd, milked twice a day. We calculated feed rations, treated sick cows with meds, bottle-fed baby calves, purchased hay and grain— there was so much to do without our daddy.

My wonderful family took a leave of absence from life as we knew it— for months on end. My husband, Irad, worked almost incessantly. Every one of my sisters and brothers-in-law spent days helping out on the farm.

With barns full of cattle, work was grueling. Scraping the barns and cleaning the stalls was a nasty business— until we sold the herd. Empty barns became clean barns. There was nothing to shovel!

In retrospect, there was no way we could have walked through those years without Divine help. The Lord carried my amazing family.

Years later, the Lord showed me His perspective.

"Without oxen a stable stays clean, but you need a strong ox for a large harvest" (Proverbs 14:4 NLT).

Translation?

"There is no milk without some manure" or "Some disturbance (manure) is the price of growth and accomplishment."

Only Time Will Tell

God's Instruction and Wisdom about Our Time on Earth

When I reminisce about growing up on our family farm, I have sweet memories of washing dishes! We always had supper with everyone at the table—at the same time.

When the meal was over, all five of us girls would help Mama clean the kitchen. We cleared the table, carried out the scraps, put up leftovers, and washed the dishes.

Two would stand at the sink, one washing dishes and the other rinsing and drying. We would laugh, make up songs, or simply finish the supper conversation. We helped out because Mama needed us to!

Today, most American families have automatic dishwashers, advertised as time savers. While automatic dishwashers are nice, they don't save time.

Time is a constant number, divided into seconds, minutes, hours, days, years. Time cannot be saved—only spent.

In the wake of timesaving appliances and electronics, family life has been sacrificed. We have become self-sufficient and don't need each other anymore to help out with essential chores.

We make a choice to do as we please without those we love the most.

The Lord teaches about time management.

> "Therefore be careful how you walk, not as unwise men but as wise, making the most of your time, because the days are evil. So then do not be foolish, but understand what the will of the Lord is" (Ephesians 5:15–17).

Fashion Sense

God's Healing, Wisdom, and Warning to be Prepared

"And whatever you do, whether in word or deed, do it all in the name of the Lord Jesus, giving thanks to God the Father through him" (Colossians 3:17 NIV).

My husband, Irad, and I saw the Lord in action at a fashion show presentation held at our reception barn on our family's small farm, Legacy Springs.

The event was sponsored to raise awareness of cancer research. An organization called Team Lexi received a portion of ticket sales for its work for children with cancer. Scripture says, "Carry each other's burdens, and in this way you will fulfill the law of Christ" (Galatians 6:2 NIV).

Sick at age six and now a beautiful teenager and one of the lovely fashion models, Lexi had been healed.

The Bible records a story of healing.

Then Jesus "took her by the hand and said to her, 'Talitha koum!' (which means 'Little girl, I say to you, get up!')" (Mark 5:41).

Following the fashion show, guests could purchase garments, and many lined up to do just that.

A reminder: the Lord instructs us to be smart fashion shoppers.

> I counsel you to buy from Me gold refined in the fire, that you may be rich; and white garments, that you may be clothed, *that* the shame of your nakedness may not be revealed; and anoint your eyes with eye salve, that you may see. (Revelation 3:18 NKJV)

Playing Hardball

God's Care, Mercy, and Victory for His Obedient Children

If you are a member of the Irad Lee family, loving baseball comes naturally!

Irad Winsette Lee Sr. was my adored father-in-law. I called him Papaw. He called me Jean-a-reno! He was mild mannered, always courteous, yet fiercely protective of his family.

He was a highly skilled builder, master carpenter, and cabinetmaker. But his pastime was baseball.

His brother Esrom pitched in local games and later became a Cleveland Indians recruit. Papaw was his catcher—a dynamic duo in the 1930s!

The baseball family tradition continued with my husband, Irad, who was a longtime coach of Dixie Youth.

Game day found the Lees on a baseball field, wherever the location.

There are many baseball memories; tall tales of games gone by. One of my most vivid recollections was a game in the early '80s when we almost became jailbirds! It was an away game—one hundred degree temperature; a local umpire called the game— and we lost a squeaker.

Post-game, tempers flared among some of our fans. Our team and fans finally departed.

The only ones remaining were our eleven-year-old daughter, Julia, Papaw, and me. We were in Papaw's car, about to pull out of the parking lot, when the umpire charged the car, yelling epithets—threatening the three of us with jail time!

Speechless, we pulled out of the parking lot. Having traveled two hundred yards on the highway, Papaw stopped in the emergency lane. He got out of the car, opened his trunk, and retrieved an object.

We resumed our trip home with his "hammer" on the seat between us. My mild-mannered father-in-law had been provoked!

I believe that Jesus, a carpenter familiar with hammers, would have understood!

"The Lord will fight for you while you keep silent" (Exodus 14:14).

Marching to Victory

God's Compassion and His Understanding of Life's Hardships

When most people recall the turbulent 1960s, they think of the Vietnam War. American soldiers were shunned when they came home. *Then,* they received no homecoming celebration for their honorable service.

The Gold Star mothers of our county decided to celebrate the local Vietnam Veterans' homecoming—more than forty years late. The organization's opinion was "better late than never." Our community concurred. A motorcade and dinner were planned for April 2014.

As my husband, Irad, and I selected a spot on the roadside for the Vietnam veteran's motorcade, I couldn't help but think back to those days of uncertainties, my high school years in the 1960s. The Vietnam War was always in the news—and always on the minds of the young men at school.

As high school students, our friends were drafted at graduation. They were trained and joined the ranks of thousands of US soldiers in Vietnam.

Following that, the worst began to happen. Many returned in coffins, having been killed in action, and funerals were planned.

My twin sister, Dean, played trumpet in the Madisonville High School band. The US Army recruited her to play taps at the funeral services. She would be positioned beyond a hill so no one could see her. Her trumpet playing was sought after, as there were so many funerals and not enough taps players.

If the Vietnam vet celebration brought forth memories for me, it surely did for the living soldiers who were honored that day—some unwelcome memories.

The Prophet Jeremiah must have had similar thoughts. Though not forsaken, Jeremiah inquired of the Lord.

"Why has my pain been perpetual and my wound incurable, refusing to be healed? Will You indeed be to me like a deceptive stream With water that is unreliable?" (Jeremiah 15:18).

Our Heavenly Father understands the grief and the sorrows of our Vietnam soldiers who waited so long for their welcome home.

He gave His Son—fallen for us.

"Surely He has borne our griefs and carried our sorrows; yet we esteemed Him stricken, smitten by God, and afflicted. But He *was* wounded for our transgressions; *He was* crushed for our iniquities; the chastisement for our peace *was* upon Him, and by His stripes we are healed" (Isaiah 53:4–5 NKJV).

Only the Lonely

God's Promises, Faithfulness, and Power in Life's Sorrows

At times in life, we find ourselves alone—not necessarily the time or the place when people are absent—just the circumstances that bring about a solitary feeling of aloneness.

These are the times we do not speak about. We simply mourn them internally.

Late into the night, the loneliness seems to enlarge, and we feel especially despondent. Fear is not our friend—fear only deepens our despondency.

The Father assures us that we are not alone.

"Though one may be overpowered by another, two can withstand him. And a threefold cord is not quickly broken" (Ecclesiastes 4:12 NKJV).

The cord of three, God the Father, Jesus the Son, and the Holy Spirit, join in the battle for our thoughts. Through belief, we join as a cord of four and the battle is won.

Jesus can be trusted in all things.

During times of desperation and doubt, we must cry out to Jesus our prayer: "... ... I do believe; help my unbelief" (Mark 9:24).

"For the word of the Lord is upright, And all His work is *done* in faithfulness" (Psalm 33:4).

When Pigs Fly

God's Faithfulness, Forgiveness, and His
Help through Life's Temptations

There were times when I was an exasperating little girl.

My headstrong ways were revealed very tellingly one evening when Mama and Daddy were hosting our preacher, his wife, and the revival staff for supper. Mama had set the dining room table, seldom used except for special occasions.

My twin sister, Dean, and I were not invited. We were fed early and sent to the bedroom. I didn't want to be banned to the bedroom, and I was miffed!

In our bedroom was a basket where our pets slept. We had begged Daddy to let us care for them—the two orphaned piglets—just while they were little.

It must have been my spitefulness that motivated me to let loose our squealing piglets, right under Mama's table, while she was serving dinner.

Entirely my idea—my sister had tried to discourage me. The adults had a chuckle and Mama handled the matter with aplomb.

I don't remember punishment, though I deserved it. Afterward, I was ashamed.

And so it is in the family of God.

The prodigal son ran through his inheritance, spending it on wild living. When he realized his mistakes, he went home in shame; yet, his father celebrated the homecoming (see Luke 15:11–32).

Through our eyes, the son deserved recrimination and punishment for his actions. But no such results are recorded in Scripture.

The aftereffect of wrongdoing is in the Father's capable hands.

"No temptation has overtaken you but such as is common to man; and God is faithful, who will not allow you to be tempted beyond what you are able, but with the temptation will provide the way of escape also, so that you will be able to endure it" (1 Corinthians 10:13).

Only when pigs fly will the Father forsake us—and that will never be!

"If we are faithless, He remains faithful, for He cannot deny Himself (2 Timothy 2:13).

A Lesson in Love

God's Exaltation, Grace, and Mercy for His Children Who Are Humble

Emptiness must have been what the Lord felt when His hometown turned Him away. It surely was His feeling when His disciples went to sleep.

How often do we go to sleep—becoming insensitive to the needs of those we love the most?

What about our own emotions?

Ever feel taken for granted, used, unwanted, or last on the list?

Jesus experienced that as well, yet He continued to love.

Remember the lepers who joyfully left without saying thanks?

If we are truthful—painful though it is—a lesson is born in standing at the back of the line. Scripture teaches that when we are invited to a banquet, we should never assume a place of honor.

> When you are invited by someone to a wedding feast, do not take the place of honor, for someone more distinguished than you may have been invited by him. If so, the host who invited both of you will come and say to you "Give this

person your seat." Then, humiliated, you will have to take the least important place. But when you are invited, take the lowest place, so that when your host comes, he will say to you, "Friend, move up to a better place." Then you will be honored in the presence of all the other guests. For all those who exalt themselves will be humbled, and those who humble themselves will be exalted. (Luke 14:8–11)

The grace of the Lord teaches humility and forgiveness. He forgives us, so we should forgive those who carelessly hurt us.

Thank you, Lord, for lessons in love.

Paying Lip Service

God's Instruction, Love, and Pardon for His Children

Those who lived through the East Tennessee blizzard of 1993 remember vividly where they were and what they were doing.

Some were trapped in the mountains, as our son Irad Lee III was, while others, like my daddy, were dealing with milk cows and power outages.

Perhaps the blizzard is the reason I forgot about him. He was a solitary old man—World War II vet, stoic, brilliant, alcoholic, a person who had endured the loss of love from some of his children. I'll call him John Doe.

The story begins seven years earlier. On February 1, 1986, in the early morning, I had lain in bed saying my generic prayers, "God bless us and protect us" (you may know the drill), when a voice, the crystal-clear voice of the Holy Spirit, spoke to me, saying, "Lord, give me the courage to witness to the one you send me today."

Startled, sitting straight up in the bed, I knew that it had not been my prayer, but that of the Lord.

I got up, and by the time I arrived for work, the prayer had slipped my mind. It was midmorning when John Doe arrived at the office. It was tough to assist him. He always preferred that a male assist him, rather than a female. On that day, he made a beeline for my office.

With a sinking feeling, I remembered the prayer and realized that John must be the one who the Lord had sent. Stumbling through the conversation, I mentioned church, and not much else.

Sporadically, over the next seven years, John would come into the office. Our discussions of faith were shallow and limited.

The day dawned about two weeks after the blizzard of '93. John visited my office and looked haggard, unkempt, and sickly. He had almost frozen in the storm. No one had checked on him.

He wanted to make sure his affairs were in order. We looked over his accounts and he left slowly. As I watched him depart through the window, the Holy Spirit once again spoke—prompting me to go after John and ask him about his salvation.

I stood as if my shoes were nailed to the floor. The Holy Spirit spoke once again and reminded me, that if I was ashamed of Jesus, Jesus would be ashamed of me. (see Luke 9:26)

I began to run—high heels and all—out the door and to John's car. His ignition was started and he was about to close his car door as I grabbed the handle.

John glanced up at me startled—his look questioning. I confessed that I had a question. Taking a deep breath, I asked "if he had ever received the Lord Jesus Christ as his personal Lord and Savior".

He immediately answered yes! He explained that he had been in a foxhole in Italy in World War II. The day prior, he had shot anything that moved—but the day following, he didn't want to even pick up his rifle.

I thanked him and he left.

It was our final conversation. John died a few days later.

Weeks passed. His son arrived at my office to settle John's affairs. I spoke of John's confession of faith. His son was incredulous—unbelieving—and quoted from Matthew 7:16, where Jesus says, "You will know them by their fruits".

We've all been guilty of judging others. At times, we've lived out our faith, paying lip service about the Lord while judging others as if we were sitting on *His* throne! The Bible warns us.

"This people honors Me with their lips. But their heart is far away from Me. But in vain do they worship Me, Teaching as doctrines the precepts of men" (Matthew 15:8–9).

Without doubt, I am convinced that I may be the only one living to have heard John's confession of faith in the Lord. I am assured that John resides in heaven, for the Word of God says "that if you confess with your mouth the Lord Jesus and believe in your heart that God has raised Him from the dead, you will be saved. For with the heart one believes unto righteousness, and with the mouth confession is made unto salvation. ... For '*whoever* calls on the name of the Lord shall be saved.'" (Romans 10:9–10, 13 NKJV emphasis added).

When God Wears Beats

God's Discipline for Disobedience and Victory for Obedience

My youth was not always fun and games! There were times when I did not obey Mama.

Asking Mama for anything while we were "in trouble" just would not do. Begging didn't work. She wouldn't listen. Disobedience carried consequences. It was as if Mama wore earplugs until I "straightened up".

Headphones, not earplugs, are required equipment today. Our grandchildren strongly advise that the Beats brand of headphones is the best!

Mama would have loved Beats!

I wonder if God, too, has Beats brand headphones and wears them at certain times, depending on who is talking.

"We know that God does not hear sinners; but if anyone is God-fearing and does His will, He hears him" (John 9:31).

The Lord loves a repentant heart. Through repentance, obedience is born.

God's victory in our lives requires obedience.

Oh, that My people would listen to Me, That Israel would walk in My ways! I would soon subdue their enemies, And turn My hand against their adversaries. The haters of the LORD would pretend submission to Him, But their fate would endure forever.

He would have fed them also with the finest of wheat;

And with honey from the rock I would have satisfied you. (Psalm 81:13–16 NKJV)

The Big Bang Theory

God's Justice for His Children

I saw a survey recently that over 50 percent of Americans have turned away from the belief that God created life (intelligent design/creationism) and have embraced the theory of evolution.

Theory is an interesting word, defined as a system of ideas explaining something; a speculative view; an idea of abstract knowledge or speculative thought.

It's also interesting that the scientific community cannot explain the inerrancy of the Bible—or the hundreds of fulfilled Bible prophecies.

Choosing the truth of God's Word over speculation seems reasonable, and yet, Supreme Court justices have ruled that American children be taught the theory of evolution in the classroom.

> And the Lord said, "Hear what the unrighteousness judge said, Now will God bring about justice for His elect who cry to Him day and night; and will He delay long over them? I tell you that He will bring about justice for them quickly. However, when the Son of Man comes, will He find faith on the earth?" (Luke 18:6–8)

Sign Language

God's Assurance of Creation and Invitation to Believe

New York, New York, is a fun place to visit in the spring! Although I am an infrequent traveler, the opportunity presented itself to accompany our grandson, Irad Lee IV, and his class on their eighth-grade trip.

As excitement for the trip mounted, we faced a dilemma. While traveling, I would miss our oldest granddaughter Katherine's *oh so important* thirteenth birthday.

Katherine's 2011 birthday occurred on Thursday—the same day we were scheduled to tour the New York headquarters of NBC News and attend their morning show.

The morning show was set up outside with guests positioned around a rectangular roped-off area. My plan was to snag an interview with the show's host and send out birthday greetings. To my dismay, other show guests had already surrounded the rope three-people deep. With my height of five feet, there was no chance to capture the eye of the host.

Plan B was to hold up a hurriedly made birthday sign. With the show on air, I moved from place to place, holding up the sign—behind very tall people—not knowing whether it was visible to the cameras and to viewers at home.

I found out the results later in an evening conversation with Julia, our daughter, who is Katherine's mother.

Though I was invisible to the TV cameras, the message celebrating Katherine's life was not. She had been delighted as she read the birthday sign many times as it *popped up* precipitously. She couldn't miss it!

There's another life-celebrating message we can't miss: the signs in the sky, the beauty of creation.

"The heavens are telling of the glory of God; And their expanse is declaring the work of His hands. Day to day pours forth speech, And night to night reveals knowledge" (Psalm 19:1–2).

The Father's message is clear. He is the life giver, He loves us, and He wants us to love Him back! Although our eyesight is limited, and we cannot see Him; He need not hold a homemade sign, for He holds the whole world in His hands. He deeply desires for us to spend life with Him—forever.

"For He is our God, And we are the people of His pasture and the sheep of His hand. Today, if you would hear His voice, Do not harden your hearts … " (Psalm 95:7–8).

Stuck in the Mud

God's Warning for Sin and Victory for Repentance

Days on the farm in the 1950s were idyllic. No place on the farm was *off limits* except during one particular summer. Daddy had dozers at work terracing the creek banks. The goal was to sow lush green grass right down to the water's edge. To dry the ground, a fresh water spring was piped to the surface. My twin sister, Dean, and I were seven.

When the dozers uncovered a nest of copperheads, Mama put her foot down. We were to steer clear of the creek unless Daddy took us.

And so he did. On one of his trips to check progress, I hitched a ride! The soil was in mounds just begging to be climbed.

I was thirsty and decided to find the newly piped spring. The ground was wet—very wet. I almost made it to the piped spring when I sank up to my knees. It was like quicksand. Losing my flip-flops in the deep mire, I couldn't move. I cried. Daddy lifted me out.

The memory is a reminder of the culture today. It's as if we have been dropped down into the mud—stuck in the filthiness of a godless society. Unless we accept the perversions, we are labeled haters. Only heaven knows how far we have fallen.

"Therefore remember from where you have fallen, and repent and do the deeds you did at first; or else I am coming to you and will remove your lampstand out of its place— unless you repent" (Revelation 2:5).

Repentance— a step in the right direction; but if you are stuck and can't step, cry out to the Father and He will do the rest.

"He lifted me out of the slimy pit, out of the mud and mire; he set my feet on a rock and gave me a firm place to stand" (Psalm 40:2 NIV).

A Bitter Pill to Swallow

God's Warning for Sin; His Invitation to Repent or Face His Wrath

As a teenage girl in the 1960s, I loved reading *Seventeen* magazine to stay in fashion and novels to stay in tune with the times.

In 1966, *Valley of the Dolls* became a best seller. The novel chronicled the rise to stardom of three women who went to New York to launch careers. They became addicted to pills—a valley of destruction. A half century later, drugs pervade our culture.

Jesus prophesied it would happen.

Sorcery (*pharmakeia*) is spoken of four times in Revelation. Translated, the Greek term means pharma or pharmacy—places where drugs are bought and sold.

A secondary meaning is poison.

His words are bitter news for unbelieving humankind.

Revelation 9:21 teaches, "And they did not repent of their murders or their sorceries [*pharmakeia*], or their sexual immorality or their thefts …" (NKJV).

And Revelation 18:23 says, "the light of a lamp will not shine in you any longer; and the voice of the bridegroom and bride will not be heard in you any longer; for your merchants were the great men of the earth, because all the nations were deceived by your sorcery [*pharmakeia*]."

There is hope.

"Therefore repent; or else I am coming to you quickly, and I will make war against them with the sword of My mouth" (Revelation 2:16).

"He who has an ear, let him hear" (Revelation 2:17).

Baby Love

God's Gift of Children; His Omnipotence and Care for the Helpless

Excitement was in the air in October 2009. Our daughter, Julia, at age thirty-eight, was expecting our sixth grandchild! It was her fourth pregnancy. This time seemed to be different from the others. Just in case, Julia kept in constant touch with her doctor.

This child was so new, with gender unknown, that discussion of names was just underway.

The baby had developed for just a few weeks when the call came. I was needed to tend the big girls, Katherine, Madi, and Lydia. Julia and our son-in-law, Shawn were headed to the hospital. Something was very wrong.

The second call came later. Julia had lost the baby.

Julia and Shawn were heartbroken.

The girls stayed with friends and us that weekend. It was Halloween. We put together costumes and went to church for treats.

Days passed. Things began to normalize, or so I thought. The onset of a migraine sent me to the therapist. Lying face down on the massage table, neck and back muscles like concrete, as the masseuse attempted to help my pain, I began crying. Big, fat tears of grief poured from my eyes, splashing onto the floor.

My body's reaction surprised me. In my thoughts, I rationalized that we had not known this unformed child—but the depths of my heart told a different story. My heart, indeed, my whole body, reacted with great pain and sorrow.

Rationalization is the danger of our society. Without the constant control of the Holy Spirit, our thoughts become desensitized—we think no child is there. Abortions and morning-after pills are commonplace.

How sad, in the Father's eyes, for "Behold, children are a gift of the Lord, The fruit of the womb is a reward" (Psalm 127:3).

The Word of God teaches of the conception of Mary's baby—our Lord Jesus. Once Mary conceived, she immediately started out on a journey. "Now at this time Mary arose and went in a hurry to the hill country to a city of Judah" (Luke 1:39).

Mary headed straightway to her cousin Elizabeth, who in her old age was also expecting a child (soon to be named John the Baptist).

Scripture does not record Mary's method of travel—perhaps walking an estimated eighty miles from Nazareth. Walking would have taken her about three days.

Upon arrival, Mary knocked on the door. " And she entered the house of Zacharias and greeted Elizabeth. When Elizabeth heard Mary's greeting, the baby leaped in her womb; and Elizabeth was filled with the Holy Spirit. And she cried out with a loud voice and said, 'Blessed *are* you among women, and blessed is the fruit of your womb! And how has it *happened* to me, that the mother of my Lord would come to me?'" (Luke 1:40–43).

Jesus' development in the womb would have been about three days, yet Elizabeth acknowledged that the days-old *fetus* was our Lord.

There is no earthly record of the baby we lost—no birth certificate nor grave. However, the Father has a record, for "nothing in all creation is hidden from God's sight" (Hebrews 4:13 NIV).

And so, to set the record straight, Irad and I have not six but a perfect seven grandchildren. Six reside on earth and one lives at home with God in heaven ... awaiting the day when we all will meet for the first time and live together forever.

We are certain our little one's soul is alive and well, for the Bible assures us,

> I was cast upon You from birth. From My mother's womb
> You *have been* My God. (Psalm 22:10 NKJV)

Pink Cadillac

God's Mercy and Healing for the Helpless and Impoverished

At age six, having teenage big sisters in the 1950s when Elvis hit the music scene was incredibly entertaining! On September 9, 1956, Mama's birthday, we gathered around the television to view *The Ed Sullivan Show* on the night Elvis made his coast-to-coast debut.

His performance of "Love Me Tender," "Hound Dog," and "Don't Be Cruel" launched Elvis's career and launched his songs to the top of the music charts.

As his stardom rose, his riches increased, though his generosity became legendary. Elvis gave hundreds of Cadillacs away. People that received his "car gifts" were in the right place at the right time.

And so was a blind man sitting beside the road as Jesus walked by—the right place at the right time. Scripture records the words.

> As Jesus approached Jericho, a blind man was sitting by the roadside begging. When he heard the crowd going by, he asked what was happening. They told him, "Jesus of Nazareth is passing by." He called out, "Jesus, Son of David, have mercy on me!" Those who led the way rebuked him and told him to be quiet, but he shouted all the more, "Son of David, have mercy on me!"

Jesus stopped and ordered the man to be brought to him. When he came near, Jesus asked him, "What do you want me to do for you?"

"Lord, I want to see," he replied. Jesus said to him, "Receive your sight; your faith has healed you." Immediately he received his sight and followed Jesus, praising God. When all the people saw it, they also praised God. (Luke 18:35–43 NIV)

Jesus is near us every moment of every day. We call out to Him— but do we hear His question: "What do you want Me to do for you?"

The next time you give the Lord a *shout out*, have your answer ready and be prepared to receive!

Well Heeled

God's Plan and Provision for the Necessary Things in Life

Those who have lived in Madisonville, Tennessee, might remember Morgan's shoe store doing business in the 1970s. Inside the store, the pungent smell of shoe-leather repair was prevalent. They sold vintage (used) shoes at bargain prices in the basement of the Kefauver Hotel Building.

In those days, I was a patron. Our budget was tight, so used shoes would do. Finding good shoes for our growing children was a challenge. An even bigger challenge was finding my size—fives. The Lord's care of our family was always apparent. We never went barefoot, unless we wanted to!

The children of Israel had a bigger problem. The wilderness had no stores! They walked out of Egypt with the clothes on their backs and the sandals on their feet. They kept on walking for forty years.

"I have led you forty years in the wilderness; your clothes have not worn out on you, and your sandal has not worn out on your foot" (Deuteronomy 29:5).

As God had instructed through Moses, the people had taken with them cast-off riches from their former Egyptian masters. "Now the sons of Israel had done according to the word of Moses, for they had requested from the Egyptians articles of silver and articles of gold, and clothing" (Exodus 12:35).

Perhaps there were children's shoes in their Egyptian booty—or just maybe the mamas had a weekly shoe swap in the desert to find the right size for their growing families.

Scripture does not tell us "how". But we know "Who" cared for them. And the results: God's provision is a sure thing.

"But if God so clothes the grass of the field, which is alive today and tomorrow is thrown into the furnace, *will* He not much more clothe you? You of little faith! Do not worry then, saying, 'What will we eat?' or 'What will we drink?' or 'What will we wear for clothing?' For the Gentiles eagerly seek all these things; for your heavenly Father knows that you need all these things. But seek first His kingdom and His righteousness, and all these things will be added to you" (Matthew 6:30–33).

Say What You Mean; Mean What You Say

God's Wisdom and His Desire that His Children Know Him

A simple pleasure is finding four-leaf clovers! My older sister Pat is the titleholder! When young, I loved picking daisies. I would pick the petals and chant, "He loves me; he loves me not." If the last petal ended in he loves me not, I would select another daisy until I got the right answer.

It's amazing how modern culture pervades our every thought, word, deed, decision—even our belief system. We casually speak seemingly innocent words and phrases repeatedly. Luck. Murphy's Law. Mother Nature.

Consider the definition of the word luck—success or failure apparently brought about by chance rather than through one's own actions.

But the Lord says "do not be deceived, God is not mocked, for whatever a man sows, this he will also reap" (Galatians 6:7).

Murphy's Law claims that anything that can go wrong will go wrong. The Bible says, "I know the plans I have for you, declares the Lord, plans to prosper you and not to harm you, plans to give you a future and a hope" (Jeremiah 29:11 NIV).

Mother Nature—no such thing. "The heavens are Yours, the earth also is Yours; the world and all it contains, You have founded them" (Psalm 89:11).

What we say really matters. "Death and life are in the power of the tongue, and those who love it will eat its fruit" (Proverbs 18:21).

Hitting the Bull's Eye

God's Instruction for Speaking and Provision for His Help

In the 1950s, Western Auto was Mama's store of choice when buying toys for special occasions. As a child, I enjoyed receiving one of those combination packages with several games—jump ropes, plastic horseshoes, and a dartboard.

Although I loved throwing darts, I never achieved success! I miss the target most every time!

Now if someone were to move the target and position it where I *aim*, I would not miss.

In the spirit world, the devil has darts— fiery ones: "withal taking up the shield of faith, wherewith ye shall be able to quench all the fiery darts of the evil one" (Ephesians 6:16 ASB).

At times we help the devil shoot. Using our tongues as a tool, we *move* the target so the devil's fiery darts hit the bull's eye.

There are many ways to move the target: repeating a lie, saying an unkind word in anger, influencing a decision that we know is wrong, failing to *be like Jesus*. It's like throwing gas on a fire in someone's life—and our own.

So also the tongue is a small part of the body, and *yet* it boasts of great things. See how great a forest is set aflame by such a small fire! And the tongue is a fire, the very world of iniquity; the tongue is set among our members as that which defiles the entire body, and sets on fire the course of *our* life, and is set on fire by hell… But no one can tame the tongue; *it is* a restless evil *and* full of deadly poison. With it we bless *our* Lord and Father, and with it we curse men, who have been made in the likeness of God; from the same mouth come *both* blessing and cursing. My brethren, these things ought not to be this way. (James 3:5–6; 8–10).

Neither bridle and bit nor rudder is needed to control the tongue; for God is ready to help.

"Set a guard over my mouth, O Lord, keep watch over the door of my lips" (Psalm 141:3).

Wedding Day Blues

God's Warning to the Church for Unpreparedness

As times have changed, Daddy's farm is no more. Irad and I were able to purchase a small part of it for our own. In recent years, we decided to name our small farm Legacy Springs. There are seasons when we host weddings on the land and enjoy the privilege of witnessing wedding celebrations!

After months of planning—music, flowers, bridal supper menu, invitations—the wedding day arrives.

The bride and her maids arrive early and style their hair and makeup. The bride dons her white wedding gown, receiving best wishes with tears of joy. She is secluded in anticipation of the hour of the groom's arrival.

He arrives. Their love relationship is apparent. It is time for the solemn occasion.

The wedding-day excitement brings to mind a future wedding: the Lord's!

Jesus is the Bridegroom; the Church is the Bride.

As the day approaches, the Church should be watching expectantly, having donned white linen robes.

However, Jesus says, "You do not know that you are wretched and miserable and poor and blind and naked" (Revelation 3:17).

Not ready? Miserable? No white robes? What is one to do?

Make right your relationship with Him.

> I pondered the direction of my life,
> and I turned to follow your laws. (Psalm 119:59 NLT)

Surrender in humility, seeking salvation.

> You will seek Me and find Me when you search for *Me* with
> all your heart. (Jeremiah 29:13)

Listen for His voice and open the door when He knocks.

> Behold, I stand at the door and knock; if anyone hears My
> voice and opens the door, I will come in to him and will
> dine with him, and he with Me. He who overcomes, I will
> grant to him to sit down with Me on My throne, as I also
> overcame. ... (Revelation 3:20–21)

Pray to overcome and get ready.

> Let us be glad and rejoice, and give honor to him: for the
> marriage of the Lamb is come, and his wife has made herself
> ready. And to her was granted that she should be arrayed
> in fine linen, clean and white: for the fine linen is the
> righteousness of saints. And he said unto me, Write, Blessed
> are they which are called unto the marriage supper of the
> Lamb. (Revelation 19:7–9 KJV)

Enjoy your wedding day!

Trivial Pursuits

God's Wisdom, Protection, and His Provision for All Things

For a child, a most treasured possession is a new bike. Many kids had one!

We had two bikes—rusting in the basement. Daddy parked them there when our older sister, Pat, wrecked and lost a front tooth. It was forbidden for any of us to ride them. We did not dare.

Apparently, there is an art to bike riding. It is something that one learns as a child and never forgets. My twin sister, Dean, learned on a family friend's bike. I did not learn.

Our children, Irad III and Julia, got bikes for Christmas at age ten. So fearful that they would become injured, I sent them to my sister Linda's home to ride.

When I was twenty-eight, Irad and our children decided to teach me. I willingly agreed to the plan—after all, how hard could it be? Most everyone had achieved the skill. My family gave me sporadic lessons at home, cheering me on. I failed to achieve the balance it took.

Not to be deterred, Irad and our kids took me next door to the Smith farm one Sunday afternoon in the summer of 1979. The dirt farm roads were deemed perfect for bike lessons. Repeatedly, I was encouraged to get up and try again—wreck after painful wreck.

That was the last day I tried. I prefer transportation with four wheels, not two! Some people are just not designed to do certain things. My nemesis is riding a bike!

Perhaps my failure was the result of not asking the Lord to help. Some might say we should not *bother* the Father with such a trivial matter. After all, He has more important things to do!

That's not the Lord I know!

God specializes in the small stuff. He loves little children—He provides guardian angels for each one!

"See that you do not despise one of these little ones, for I say to you that their angels in heaven continually see the face of My Father who is in heaven" (Matthew 18:10).

He created ants and gave them wisdom.

> Four things on earth are small, yet they are extremely wise:
> Ants are creatures of little strength, yet they store up their food in the summer;
> hyraxes are creatures of little power, yet they make their home in the crags;
> locusts have no king, yet they advance together in ranks;
> a lizard can be caught with the hand, yet it is found in kings' palaces. (Proverbs 30:24–28 NIV)

He makes beauty out of evil, giving mercy to the undeserving. He desires to hold us close. He is interested in our every thought, every action, every success, every failure (including bike riding).

Is the Lord involved in what we might consider *trivial pursuits?*

Absolutely!

"And my God will supply all your needs according to His riches in glory in Christ Jesus" (Philippians 4:19).

Blinded by the Light

God's Deliverance and Promise of Abundant Life

Summertime in 1962. Madisonville Drive-in was in full swing. A feature film was showing.

My sisters and I counted the minutes until dusk. Finally, it was time to leave for the movie. Mama was driving. Our older sister, Linda, called front seat, and my twin sister, Dean, and I took the back. Excited to fever pitch, Dean and I would have ridden in the trunk if necessary (some did!).

Daddy did not accompany us. He had left for a meeting at the home of his good friend and Monroe County Sheriff, Howard Kirkpatrick.

As we headed to the drive-in, we passed the sheriff's house on College Street and saw Daddy's car backing out of the driveway.

Darkness was descending. We couldn't see Daddy in the car, but we waved anyway!

When we arrived home from the movie, Daddy was waiting up. He was glad to see us and inquired about the movie. He patiently listened as we described every action scene.

Once our excitement fizzled out, Daddy told us he had caught a ride home from the sheriff. He had assumed we had borrowed his car.

The truth dawned. While on the road, we had witnessed thieves stealing Daddy's car right out of the sheriff's driveway. Because we could not see in the darkness, no rescue occurred.

The truth dawned on Saul, too, while on the road to Damascus. Though Saul was religious, his life was in darkness until Jesus came to his rescue. Scripture records Saul's (Paul) eyewitness account:

> 'While so engaged as I was journeying to Damascus with the authority and commission of the chief priests, at midday, O King, I saw on the way a light from heaven, brighter than the sun, shining all around me and those who were journeying with me. And when we had all fallen to the ground, I heard a voice saying to me in the Hebrew dialect 'Saul, Saul, why are you persecuting Me? It is hard for you to kick against the goads.' And I said, 'Who are You, Lord?' And the Lord said, 'I am Jesus whom you are persecuting. But get up and stand on your feet; for this purpose I have appeared to you, to appoint you a minister and a witness not only to the things which you have seen, but also to the things in which I will appear to you; rescuing you from the *Jewish* people and from the Gentiles, to whom I am sending you, to open their eyes so that they may turn from darkness to light and from the dominion of Satan to God, that they may receive forgiveness of sins and an inheritance among those who have been sanctified by faith in Me.' (Acts 26:12-18)

Living in darkness is perilous. Jesus rescues the perishing, exchanges darkness for light, and gives life in abundance to those who are willing.

'The thief comes only to **steal** and kill and destroy; I came that they may have life, and have *it* abundantly.' (John 10:10)

146

A Picture Is Worth a Thousand Laughs

God's Love, Wisdom, and Understanding

There is nothing more uncomfortable than being tickled in church. I guess everybody has done that at some time.

There have been several such occasions in my life, but I remember one time vividly.

Our children were small. Irad and I had chosen a pew in the back of church. Irad III was six years old, Julia four. We had entertained them with surprises from my bag, but we had run out of tricks.

Although I had very little artistic talent, to entertain the kids, I drew pictures on the bulletin. The children had grown tired of my square-house-with-chimney pictures.

After motioning for Irad to give me a rest, I handed him paper and pen. He went to work.

Both children watched intently as their daddy drew a picture. I turned my attention to the sermon.

Hearing the beginning of laughter from the kids, I looked over to take a peek. Irad's art talents rivaled mine—almost nonexistent! What I saw was a drawing of the funniest man I had ever seen.

The laugh started deep within, and then encompassed me. Slapping my hand to my mouth, I looked over at Irad's grin, and I *lost it*. The whole pew shook until our laughter erupted.

All four of us made our escape, trying to hurry as if something were amiss. People around us looked on with concern.

Some might say that our laughter was inappropriate. Perhaps, but that day was so joyful—I loved the Lord for understanding.

"A merry heart does good, *like* medicine, But a broken spirit dries the bones" (Proverbs 17:22 NKJV).

Cut to the Chase

God's Love of Children and Faithfulness to Answer Prayer

The car games that we learn as children are great fun! On a trip a few years ago, I found myself driving to Pigeon Forge, Tennessee, with two of our grandchildren, Irad IV and Madi. They were just the perfect age to play a car game, so we made one up.

Each of us selected a color and counted the oncoming vehicles matching our color. The first player to reach twenty vehicles was the victor in the game. Silver, white, and black were the big winners of the day—bright colors the losers!

On the return trip, Irad and Madi asked to play our car game again. I readily agreed, but since we had taken a shortcut through the country, "car action" was sparse at best. And to make matters worse, Irad's color was orange and Madi's yellow.

We traveled for forty-five minutes, not meeting a single car. Approaching a four-lane highway, and knowing we would meet more cars, I tried to resurrect their interest in the game. They both said it was hopeless. I suggested that they ask Jesus to play with them and supply orange and yellow vehicles.

Madi questioned whether Jesus would really want to play. Remembering what Jesus said, 'Permit the children to come to me, and do not hinder them …'" (Luke 18:16); I reassured them that Jesus loved being involved in every part of their lives.

Irad and Madi agreed to pray. I breathed my own prayer, asking Jesus to show them His glory.

As we entered the four-lane highway, traffic was very heavy. Irad and Madi were watching intently in anticipation of who would be the victor. We were almost out of time, minutes away from our destination. There it was at the red light—a big *orange* Dodge truck! It would appear that Irad was the winner—except there was a little *yellow* Mini Cooper sitting beside the truck in the next lane. Wow!

The children were delighted that they were both winners. I was amazed at the Lord's faithfulness.

Jesus take the wheel!

Holy Cow

God's Watchfulness and Help for His Children

Growing up on a dairy farm, there was always that inconvenient time when the cows got out. Our family would put them up, night or day, rain or shine. My husband, Irad, and I lived down the road from Daddy, and there were many times through the years when we were "on call" when the cows got out.

One of those times was a cold winter Sunday night. We had experienced unresolved drainage damage from a neighboring development. It had rained for days. The ground was saturated. Irad was *not* a happy camper to say the least, and he had been sick for days with the flu.

It was I who discovered them—Daddy's herd of heifers standing in our yard, hoofs sinking deep into the soil. Irad knew something was wrong when I awakened him and asked him where he stored his wire cutters.

I thought my plan was a good one—to cut the fence and herd them into the field behind our house. I gingerly broke the news about the herd of heifers standing in our yard.

My attempt to avert Irad's reaction was to no avail. His temper ignited. He was ready to do harm that night. Sick as he was, he stormed out of the house into the pouring rain. He told me to stay put!

In the dark and rain, he found the fence break (the posts had loosened due to excess drainage), herded the heifers into the field, drove the posts, then got into his truck and headed to town to confront the developer. I knew that if the person Irad went to see was at home, with Irad being so angry—it wouldn't end well.

My prayer is vivid still today.

"Jesus, send help. Irad's in trouble. Send help now!"

Later Irad returned, and he calmly told me an amazing story.

Having driven only a half mile up Hiwassee Road, he had seen a curious site. A lone cow was standing on the edge of the road. Irad knew that was odd… cows usually stay with the herd. And stranger still, it was a dairy cow, not a heifer! He was afraid a car would hit the cow and cause a wreck so he stopped to put up the cow. Aware that a single cow, apart from a herd, could be temperamental, Irad went to Daddy's barn to get one of the men to help.

Minutes later, the men returned to the road at the place where the cow had been standing. The cow was gone. In disbelief, Irad assured his helper it had been there. Time went by as they searched along the fence in the rain and darkness, up and down the road.

Irad was convinced he had seen it. But the cow had vanished. Amazed, he got into his truck. His anger had passed. The Lord had intervened on his behalf.

Inexplicable? Yes! However, Irad will confess that the help Jesus sent was a *holy cow*!

"There is none like the God of Jeshurun, Who rides the heavens to your help, And through the skies in His majesty" (Deuteronomy 33:26).

Thanks Living

God's Recognition and Salvation for His Children Who Give Thanks

Southerners have a distinctive way of expressing themselves. For thank you, we say appreciate it. Or much obliged. Or many thanks.

Parents everywhere teach children to say thank you as courtesy. It is the proper discipline.

When we were growing up in our home, being discourteous had consequences! Mama wouldn't tolerate an ungrateful attitude!

Recall the lepers that Jesus healed? Only two out of ten went back to thank the Lord. Their story made it into the Bible.

Gratitude is very important to the Lord. In fact, God calls it a sacrifice.

"Oh that *men* would praise the Lord *for* His goodness, and *for* His wonderful works to the children of men! And let them sacrifice the sacrifices of thanksgiving, and declare His works with rejoicing" (Psalm 107:21–22 NKJV).

Jesus gave thanks for the bread when feeding the crowds. It's amazing to me that the creator of all things would give thanks.

Jesus knew how to sacrifice!

The sacrifice of thanksgiving is manifested in many ways: in person or by praise, prayer, purity, possessions.

It pleases the Father when we exhibit a grateful heart.

"He who offers a sacrifice of thanksgiving honors Me; And to him who orders *his* way *aright* I shall show the salvation of God" (Psalm 50:23).

It's a Mad Mad Mad Mad World

God's Blessings for Generosity, Obedience, and Pleasing Him

Movie makers in 1963 brought us an action comedy using the dying words of a thief to spark a *madcap* cross-country rush to find treasure.

Purportedly, during the Civil War, our family farm was the site of a Yankee campground, located at the headwaters of Bat Creek near the old McCrosky house. Hobbyists have used metal detectors to search the farm for Yankee gold coins.

I have fleetingly considered the purchase of a metal detector, hoping to locate a cache of hidden gold. It's intriguing: the thought of finding lost treasure!

And if found—what to do with it?

The Lord tells us.

"But store up for yourselves treasures in heaven, where neither moth nor rust destroys, and where thieves do not break in or steal, for where your treasure is, there your heart will be also" (Matthew 6:20–21).

How do we *deposit* treasure in heaven?

"Command them to do good, to be rich in good deeds, and to be generous and willing to share. In this way they will lay up treasure for themselves as a firm foundation for the coming age, so that they may take hold of the life that is truly life" (1 Timothy 6:18–19 NIV).

The Father pays attention to our "heavenly deposits" of helping the poor and praying for them.

"Your prayers and gifts to the poor have come up as a memorial offering before God" (Acts 10:4 NIV).

The Green Green Grass of Home

God's Grace and Mercy

Mowing is our summer pastime. My husband, Irad requires *grace* from the Lord when I operate mowing equipment. He is torn between being fearful I will become injured and being afraid of what I'll *tear up!*

We've resided at the same address since our marriage in 1968. Initially we lived in a mobile home. To embellish our *humble abode*, Irad made a gravel path and built a small front porch. He painted the porch white, and I planted a bed of scarlet sage and petunias at the steps. At that time, we had only a half-acre to mow.

Home alone, I decided to use Daddy's powerful riding mower to *trim*— just the edge of the lawn along the front of the mobile home. Sitting on the mower, easing carefully, with perfect alignment, I reached the porch and stopped. I needed to back up. Unfamiliar with Daddy's mower, I was certain that *reverse* was engaged. I hit the throttle. The mower lunged forward. Daddy's mower proved to be powerful, as advertised— shoving the porch several feet!

The doorknob stopped the porch from moving further.

Reverse located, I backed out, parked the mower, and went inside to wait for Irad.

From the window, I watched his arrival. He stepped onto the porch and reached for the doorknob. That's when he realized—

Grace and mercy abounded! As I remember, Irad laughed, fixed the porch, and reminded me, with wise instruction, that push mowers are to be used for trimming.

Years later, I have learned not to *go it alone.* The Lord gives instruction and shows grace and mercy in every situation, for our Savior says,

"Therefore let us draw near with confidence to the throne of grace, so that we may receive mercy and find grace to help in time of need." (Hebrews 4:16)

Family Jewels

God's Love of Family and Provision of Comfort and Deliverance

There are seasons in life that are painful; 1988 was a really hard year.

It was a year of goodbyes for Irad Lee Sr. (Irad's daddy), Georgie Tate Lee (Irad's mama), Dorothy Hambaugh (Irad's sister), Brent Abbott (my twin sister's husband), and extended family members Buster Orman and P. C. Hambaugh, Sr. All were deeply loved, their departure painful. All had left for heaven by autumn of 1988.

In October 1989, the Lee family decided to spend time together. Perhaps it was a yearning to reunite after a year of grief. A weeklong trip to the Gulf Coast sounded like a bit of heaven on earth; indeed, it was, for the family members who could schedule the time away.

The week began with great fun. Days were spent on the beach or golf course—except for the day we all spent at the hospital.

Irad's brother, David, developed chest pains and was feared to have had a heart attack. We filled the small hospital waiting room until the doctor relented and allowed *all* of us in to see David.

Laughter from David's room echoed down the hall. The merriment was contagious.

Medical tests had confirmed a false alarm. David was good to go!

I remember watching the banter when Irad and his sisters, Janie, Barbara, Ann, and Sara, surrounded David's bed for a last *photo memento* before leaving the hospital.

It's a memory I will forever cherish—observing these members of my husband's family, as precious as jewels to me. The greatest assurance is that, as believers in Jesus, we will know each other forever, no matter where we reside, whether on earth or in heaven.

God has promised and I believe!

"The Lord their God will save his people on that day as a shepherd saves his flock. They will sparkle in his land like jewels in a crown" (Zechariah 9:16 NIV).

God's Hope for His Children to Be Like Christ

New Year's Eve will find the Lee family playing cards. Friendly competition is combined with lots of laughter!

One of our card games involves *sticking* an unknown card to each person's forehead. Everyone can see the front of the card except the player himself. Every player can read the others' cards.

It's a blast to play—not knowing which card appears on your forehead.

It reminds me of a headband logo, positioned so that others can *read* your forehead!

The concept is not a product of modern marketing. The idea of headband names was originated by the One and Only!

Design. Color. Chosen by God.

"You shall also make a plate of pure gold and shall engrave on it, like the engravings of a seal, 'Holy to the Lord.' ... ... You shall fasten it on a blue cord, and it shall be on the turban; it shall be at the front of the turban. It shall be on Aaron's forehead, and Aaron shall take away the iniquity of the holy things which the sons of Israel consecrate, with regard to all their holy gifts; and it shall always be on his forehead, that they may be accepted before the Lord" (Exodus 28:36–39).

Ancient priests are not the only ones assigned to wear the engraving; believers in Christ are priests, also.

"and He has made us *to be* a kingdom, priests to His God and Father— to Him *be* the glory and the dominion forever and ever. Amen" (Revelation 1:6).

Consider the reaction if everyone could see the *priestly* inscription "Holy to the Lord" written on our foreheads!

Perhaps the words we speak would be chosen more carefully or our actions tempered with love.

The King of Kings has chosen us and assigned us to be like Him.

Holy. Holy. Holy.

Fish Out of Water

God's Instruction to Witness for Jesus

All it takes to have a great fishing adventure can be found at Legacy Springs, our small family farm. It's endowed with a two-acre lake stocked with a variety of fish, compliments of the local fish wagon. The lake is equipped with a fishing dock and the farmland is enriched with plenty of worm bait.

We had aspirations that *all* of our grandchildren would love fishing—and they do fish on occasion. Madi emerged as a natural. Her family claim to fame was being the first and (so far) the last to catch a catfish. When she was age twelve, before her rigorous high school days, her rod, reel, and tackle box stood ready. She would go fishing whenever she was visiting.

Scripture speaks of fishermen. The Lord's disciples fished as expert professionals at the Sea of Galilee.

Jesus changed their style of fishing.

"'Come, follow me,' Jesus said, 'and I will send you out to fish for people'" (Matthew 4:19 NIV).

The disciples didn't need a boat or nets to fish Jesus' way. Their simple requirement was obedience and the power of the Holy Spirit.

"But you will receive power when the Holy Spirit comes on you; and you will be my witnesses in Jerusalem, and in all Judea and Samaria, and to the ends of the earth" (Acts 1:8 NIV).

It is time to go fishing!

Witness Protection

God's Promise of Freedom and Protection

We are a movie-watching family! As new releases hit the market, we go to the movie store to make our selections.

In 1994, John Grisham's suspense thriller *The Client* hit the big screen. As the story unfolded, two adolescent brothers heard a crime confession that implicated the mob.

The street-smart older brother (age thirteen) recognized that his family needed help as both the FBI and mobsters chased him. The film ended as the two boys and their mother flew off into the sunset, having been admitted into the Witness Protection Program.

Developed in the early 1970s, the US Witness Protection Program involves people implicated to have knowledge of crimes. They testify to the truth for protection.

After the trial, with new identities, the witnesses—under government protection—live out the remainder of their lives in a different location. If they live within the rules with their new identities, the government reports, there is a 100 percent survival rate.

Witness protection is not an original concept of the US Government; the government apparently made variations to the Lord's witness protection program.

Though innocent, Jesus went through two trials. He could have implicated us.

"For all have sinned and fall short of the glory of God" (Romans 3:23).

Jesus never testified.

"He was oppressed (brutally tortured) and afflicted, yet He did not open *His* mouth" (Isaiah 53:7, emphasis added).

He received the death penalty.

"Then Pilate turned Jesus over to them to be crucified" (John 19:16 NLT).

Believers in Jesus are given immunity for *life*—with a 100 percent survival rate. No one protected is ever lost.

"For the law of the Spirit of life in Christ Jesus has set you free from the law of sin and of death" (Romans 8:2).

Believers have new identities, marked by the Holy Spirit; Our witness of truth occurs after the trial.

"For this I have been born, and for this I have come into the world, to testify to the truth. Everyone who is of the truth hears My voice" (John 18:37).

And Jesus says, "Go into all the world and proclaim the gospel to the whole creation" (Mark 16:15 NIV).

Praise to the Skies

God's Goodness; Our Hope and Praise

Music is embedded in my family's heritage. Mama and Daddy's families produced singers, pianists, organists, and other instrumentalists.

When I was a child in the 1950s, Mama's yearly Jordan family reunions inspired in me a fever-pitch anticipation of joy. Mama grew up in a large family. At the reunions, laughter was the recipe of the day, though food was abundant, served on long tables in the yard. It was almost impossible to decide which to choose—Aunt Audra Sexton's or Aunt Mildred Jordan's chicken and dumplings!

When dinner was finished, strains of music—favorite songs, many of them gospel songs—could be heard. Mama's sister and brother, Aunt Mary Blake and Uncle "Lidge" (Elijah) Jordan, played the banjo. Mama set the rhythm by playing the *spoons,* as we sang along.

My sisters inherited musical ability. Nancy, my oldest sister, played the piano for almost a lifetime, starting in a small church as a teenager. That began her lifelong mission—offering the sacrifice of praise to the Lord. She played piano and organ in churches wherever she lived.

In March 2013, Nancy became very ill, almost to the point of death. I visited her on a rainy spring night. We spoke about her imminent departure for heaven. I asked if she was afraid. Breathless and weak, her answer was simple, "To live is Christ—to die is gain" (Philippians 1:21).

On April 10, 2013, she left for heaven.

I had once inquired of Nancy her favorite Bible passage. She said it was Psalm 52. Later, I read Psalm 52 and knew that without a doubt the words written there were her tribute and lifelong witness to the Lord.

King David was like minded:

"For what you have done I will always praise you in the presence of your faithful people. And I will hope in your name, for your name is good" (Psalm 52:9 NIV).

Love You to the Dump

God's Everlasting Love and Forgiveness

Bedtime at our home in the 1970s was chaotic. Story time was never a calming activity for our sleepy eyed children. Their dad, my husband, Irad, did not read a favorite story—*he made them up*!

The giggles coming from the bedrooms of our children, Irad III and Julia, made settling them down for sleep a little bit harder. Missing the goal for bedtime was a common occurrence—and yet those moments created sweet, carefree memories of bedtimes past.

Our daughter, Julia, has carried on with her daddy's love of bedtime stories. She developed her own bedtime story favorites when her girls were small. Her youngest, Annalee, as a three-year-old, was introduced to Julia's favorite story called "Love You to the Moon and Back." Hearing the story is at the top of Annalee's favorite activities—right up there with taking the trash to the dump (our Southern version of a convenience center).

Following a full day of activities, which included a trip to the dump with her dad, Annie was a sleepy eyed little girl. Julia tucked her in at bedtime with the words "Love you to the moon and back."

Annalee responded by giving her mother a huge hug and proclaiming, "I love you to the dump!"

God feels the same. He loves us in spite of the sin in our lives.

We miss the mark of God's righteousness every single day. He yearns to rid us of the filth that makes us stumble—impure thoughts, wrong motives, unrighteous actions.

The Father is pleased when we take our sin to Him through confession and leave it behind. And in so doing, we create sweet memories of *His* faithfulness.

Have you ever speculated on how the Father disposes of the sin we leave behind?

The answer is simple. He dumps it into the sea!

> He will again have compassion on us;
> He will tread our iniquities under foot.
> Yes, You will cast all their sins
> Into the depths of the sea. (Micah 7:19)

Glory Be

God's Plan and Help for His Children of Glory

A popular TV show in the 1960s, hosted by Art Linkletter, was *House Party*. With hilarity, we watched his guest interviews of young children with unpredictable answers! One of Art's questions was "What do you want to *be* when you grow up"?

It's age old—the quest for life's meaning. Many believers in Christ have searched for the answer, as is demonstrated by the popularity of self-help guides to growing one's faith.

The Bible gives us answers.

He equips us.

"… … … equip you with everything good for doing his will, and may he work in us what is pleasing to him, through Jesus Christ, to whom be glory forever and ever. Amen" (Hebrews 13:21 NIV).

He lets us choose.

"Whatever you do, do your work heartily, as for the Lord rather than for men, knowing that from the Lord you will receive the reward of the inheritance. It is the Lord Christ whom you serve" (Colossians 3:23–24).

He wants us to be content with His provision.

"Keep your lives free from the love of money and be content with what you have, because God has said, 'Never will I leave you; never will I forsake you'" (Hebrews 13:5 NIV).

Our life purpose?

To *be* His glory:

"Do not fear, for I have redeemed you; I have called you by My name, you are Mine! … Everyone who is called by My Name and whom I have created for *My Glory*, Whom I have formed, even whom I have made" (Isaiah 43:1, 7, emphasis added).

A Family Tradition

God's Promise of Love and Help of the Holy Spirit

Bandages have come a long way from the generic kind of the 1970s. Back then, our daughter, Julia, *always* wore one. The tradition must be ingrained in our DNA. All of her girls wear them whether needed or not.

Mothers everywhere can identify with the satisfaction of watching their godly daughters rear children by putting band-aids on skinned knees and balm on hurt feelings. Having a front-row seat to observe Julia becoming a mother *four times* has been a blessing.

Birthing babies, however painful and miraculous, is the easy part. Julia's investment in her daughters' spiritual birth—receiving the Lord and Savior—is her greatest feat. She has done that, continuing to impart the fruit of the Spirit.

"But the fruit of the Spirit is love, joy, peace, forbearance, kindness, goodness, faithfulness, gentleness and self-control" (Galatians 5:22–23 NIV).

The love of the Lord is a family tradition. Thousands of generations of families have experienced it, though not by accident. It's in their DNA—being a part of the family of God. His love has been experienced and imparted by faithful parents down through the ages. It's the kind of family that I know and give thanks for.

"You shall not make for yourself an image in the form of anything in heaven above or on the earth beneath or in the waters below. You shall not bow down to them or worship them; for I, the Lord your God, am a jealous God, punish the children for the sin of the parents to the third and fourth generation of those who hate me, but showing love to a thousand generations of those who love me and keep my commandments" (Deuteronomy 5:8–10 NIV).

God's Encouragement and Provision for Families

It was a privilege to be mentored and mothered by two wonderful and beloved women, my mother, Katherine Elizabeth Howard, *and* my mother-in-law, Georgie Lee, who I called Nanaw.

Both possessed qualities of godliness, perseverance, nobility.

A passage from the Bible best describes them (I have paraphrased from Proverbs).

> Strength and dignity were their clothing, and they laughed at the time to come. They opened their mouths with wisdom, and the teaching of kindness was on their tongue. They looked well to the ways of their household and did not eat the bread of idleness. Their children rise up and called them blessed; their husbands also, and they praised them: "Many women have done excellently, but they surpassed them all" (Proverbs 31:25–30).

Mama was my confidant, mentor, and beloved friend until her accident. I met Nanaw at age sixteen when Irad and I were dating in high school. Remarkably, I knew them both for twenty-three very short years.

Final exchanged embraces and goodbyes were not possible for either. Mama departed instantly in a car wreck. Fourteen years later, Nanaw left after a debilitating stroke—leaving her unable to communicate.

As Jesus, on the cross in agony, remembered His earthly mother and gave her another son, He saw my agony and gave me Nanaw as a mother for a time. (Compare John 19:26–27.)

At age thirty-nine— in their absence, I experienced trepidation and fear, wondering if I was prepared to be the *go to* person. Was I wise enough? Had I learned my lessons well enough to continue without them? Only by the Lord's mercy and grace was that possible.

It has been many years since Mama and Nanaw left for heaven. My best memories were of both laughing!

The greatest lesson came not from their presence but their absence— as I try to live out the days with no regrets, to cherish those given to me, and to prepare for life everlasting, which is the ultimate goal for my household and me.

By the Book

God's Plan and Inspired Word for Our Good

One of the most difficult tasks is sorting through the treasures of a lifetime of a beloved family member. Tender moments are spent remembering—then making the decisions. Who gets what?

When Nanaw (Georgie Tate Lee), my husband's mama, left for heaven, the house was replete with memorabilia and priceless items.

Irad's oldest brother, Alton, and his wife, Jewel, lived on the West Coast and were not able to travel to East Tennessee. Alton had sent word that he was content—and not to worry about including him in the sharing of his mother's personal items.

The family thought differently and sent Alton the most treasured item of all: Nanaw's Bible. Though he had not expected the Bible in the mail and apparently was caught *off guard*, Alton called when he received the package. He asked, "What am I supposed to do with it?"

The reply was, "Read it!"

The Bible, a worldwide best seller since it was first printed, is *not* just a book.

"In the beginning was the Word, and the Word was with God, and the Word was God. He was in the beginning with God" (John 1:1–2).

The Word and God are one—but there's *more.*

"And the Word became flesh, and dwelt among us, and we saw His glory, glory as of the only begotten from the Father, full of grace and truth" (John 1:14).

The Word and Jesus are one. Yet *more still.*

"Man shall not live on bread alone, but on every word that comes from the mouth of God" (Matthew 4:4).

Jesus imparts life through the Word.

"So faith *comes* from hearing, and hearing by the word of Christ" (Romans 10:17).

"Make them holy by your truth; teach them your word, which is truth" (John 17:17 NLT).

Assurances of *faith, truth, holiness,* and *life* are obtained from knowing the Word of God. The Bible—the Word of God—is *not just a book.*

Alton and Jewell can testify. They read, believed, and live by the Book! Their reward from the Lord is prepared. They are counted among those who have loved His appearing.

"in the future there is laid up for me the crown of righteousness, which the Lord, the righteous Judge, will award to me on that day; and not only to me, but also to all who have loved His appearing" (2 Timothy 4:8).

Bridging the Gap

God's Strength, Power, Defense, and Inheritance for His Anointed

In the 1950s, going to Grandma's house, Daddy's childhood home, was a journey we looked forward to! We anticipated with pleasure seeing our beloved grandparents, Walter and Hattie Jane Howard. And the trip to get there was itself a great adventure.

No fast food restaurants were available. Mama would pack a picnic lunch and we would eat at the roadside.

Timing our departure was important. We had to meet the Washington Ferry at its crossing site. Established in the 1800s, it was one of the few ferry crossings for the Tennessee River.

Once across, we drove on down the highway to a country road in northern Hamilton County. Almost there, we forded a tributary of Sale Creek. With squeals of laughter coming from the back seat, Daddy literally drove the car right through the water!

Through a six-year-old's eyes, the trip sometimes held perils. On stormy days, the ferry crossing was rough. And if spring rains brought high water, we weren't able to ford the creek! Daddy always got us through, though, and back home safe and sound!

It is extraordinary—we did not cross a single bridge to go home!

Home. It's a comforting word. Our Heavenly Father has planned a home for us. God calls it the Promised Land.

The story of Israelites' deliverance out of Egypt to the land of Canaan, the Promised Land, involved a seemingly impossible journey. There were *no* bridges. The Israelites relied on God to part the Red Sea and later, the flooding Jordan River, so they could get to their new home. (see Exodus 14 and Joshua 3)

Symbolically speaking, for those who want to go to the Father's heavenly home, there is one more river to cross—the River Jordan.

And there remains no need for a bridge! Those who love the Lord Jesus need not fret—the One who walks on water will *carry* us over.

"Blessed be the Lord, Because He has heard the voice of my supplication. The Lord is my strength and my shield; My heart trusts in Him, and I am helped; Therefore my heart exults, And with my song I shall thank Him. The Lord is their strength, And He is a saving defense to His anointed. Save Your people and bless Your inheritance; Be their shepherd also, and carry them forever" (Psalm 28:6–9).

War and Peace

God's Abiding Peace Given to His Children

Sometimes being with the right people when your heart is sad is balm for the soul. My husband, Irad, his sister, Sara, and I slipped away for a much-needed sabbatical.

Sara arranged impressive accommodations. The richly appointed beachfront condo was of penthouse quality.

The year, 1988, had been incredibly painful and exhausting, leading to wounded hearts from sorrow and grief. Too many loved ones had said their goodbyes, too soon.

During our trip, we were as the Three Musketeers: comrades in arms, having made it through a war. Our weaponry was the sword—the Word of God. Many battles had been fought: contending with fear and dread, holding on to hope, and embracing faith in God.

We were soul weary.

Our quest was peace. Our unspoken cry: One for all and all for one.

Jesus was the realization of our cry. He exemplified our hope and justified our faith.

"For the love of Christ controls us, having concluded this, that one died for all, therefore all died; and He died for all, so that they who live might no longer live for themselves, but for Him who died and rose again on their behalf" (2 Corinthians 5:14–15).

As our days together ended, we packed our bags and headed home. Laughter had replaced sorrow. We made sad faces "just for fun", not desiring our time together to end.

Faithfully Jesus had come to our rescue. The Lord was within our midst that week—and had fulfilled our deepest need.

"He will redeem my soul in peace from the battle *which is* against me ..." (Psalm 55:18).

I Want to Go Home

God's Gentleness, Compassion, and Love for His Children

Cold, wintry days evoke memories of Grandma's house. Living on their farm in Sale Creek, Tennessee, Grandma and Grandpa, Hattie and Walter Howard, welcomed us for visits.

Shortly after Daddy's near-fatal car wreck, Mama and Daddy had travel plans related to Daddy's convalescence. So they took my twin sister, Dean, and I to Grandma's for a few days. We were six years old.

With plenty of girl cousin playmates, Grandma's good country cooking, and exploration on the farm, I should have been content.

The first night was very cold. Grandma tucked four of us girls into the same bed. There was no central heat. The quilts, piled high, were so heavy that we coordinated rolling over all at one time!

My tears began on day two. I was homesick. Sweet Grandma pulled me onto her lap—and rocked me for the remainder of the week.

Gentleness and compassion abounded; never a cross word did she speak.

The Lord Jesus is like that. "He felt compassion for them, because they were distressed and dispirited like sheep without a shepherd" (Matthew 9:36).

"… He will gently lead the nursing ewes" (Isaiah 40:11).

I still get homesick and sometimes yearn for home in heaven. My room there is under construction.

"The Lord is preparing a place for me" (John 14:3, my paraphrase)

Until then,

> The Lord's lovingkindnesses indeed never cease. For His compassions never fail. They are new every morning. Great is Your faithfulness. (Lamentations 3:22–23)

Keep On Trucking

God's Encouragement for His Children Who Please Him

By the mid-1960s, Mama and Daddy switched from raising eighty thousand broiler chickens to twenty thousand laying hens. They retooled the chicken houses, Mama hired a crew of women, and the result was a superabundance of eggs!

We had a refrigerated panel truck for delivering eggs. Daddy would haul eggs once a week on daylong runs to Abbington, Virginia. Mama was apprehensive that Daddy would fall asleep while driving; she made sure that either my twin sister, Dean, or I accompanied him. I do not remember when we learned to drive, but by the time we were sixteen, Dean and I had plenty of experience.

We started early on delivery day. The trip, one way, took four hours. Coming home from egg delivery, Daddy would invariably ask me to drive so that he could sleep.

One day, I was at the wheel. Nearing home, as we approached the Little Tennessee River Bridge, I awakened Daddy to drive us on in. I was petrified to cross the narrow bridge driving our wide, unwieldy truck!

Daddy encouraged me to go on, saying, "I could make it". And he closed his eyes again. I drove the truck across the narrow bridge without mishap. Those in the line of vehicles behind us were glad!

Once we were across the river, Daddy, apparently having been aware of my every move, said I did a good job, adding, "That wasn't so bad after all."

I agreed with him … saying that it helped when I closed my eyes!

Life is so like that. Dreading what is ahead, we close our eyes, fearful of failure.

With closed eyes and darkness all around, we shut out the light, *His light.*

For Jesus said, "I am the Light of the world; he who follows Me will not walk in the darkness, but will have the Light of life" (John 8:12).

We have life in Him. So what should we do if there is *dread ahead?*

Trust the Father and keep on going, for His Word says,

> So if you are suffering in a manner that pleases God, keep on doing what is right, and trust your lives to the God who created you, for he will never fail you. (1 Peter 4:19 NLT)

The Bucket List

God's Love for the Lost and Assurance of Redemption

In 2008, Hollywood produced the movie *The Bucket List*. Two terminally ill men escape from a cancer ward and head off on a road trip with a wish list of things to do before they die.

One thing on my own bucket list was relearning how to can vegetables. Though it was not very exciting and I was unable to explain why I wanted to recapture the skill, it was something I decided to do.

I had learned from the best! When canning, Nanaw, Irad's mother, used the water-bath method. She wouldn't let me buy a pressure canner to use; she said I was too *harem scarem* and I would blow my head off! Because of my love for her and my complete obedience, *I believed her*, always using water to can—never a pressure canner!

That was many years ago.

In recent years, we grew a garden. As I used Nanaw's methods of long ago, canned salsa and spaghetti sauce appeared on our shelves. With jars and lids washed clean and made sterile, the sounds of pop, pop, pop assured safety from contamination. Each jar was sealed.

The fruit of my labor would fly off the shelf. My family enjoyed every bite.

The Lord approved of the work for He says, "When you shall eat of the fruit of your hands, You will be happy and it will be well with you" (Psalm 128:2).

There's one thing left in my bucket. Epaphras had it in his *bucket* too.

"Epaphras, who is one of your number, a bondslave of Jesus Christ, sends you his greetings, always laboring earnestly for you in his prayers, that you may stand perfect and fully assured in all the will of God" (Colossians 4:12).

Not by me, but by God's grace, there dwells in my soul a yearning for family, friends, and strangers to join the family of God—washed clean, exemplifying love and obedience to Jesus as believers through faith, safe from destruction through the work of the Holy Spirit, and *"sealed unto the day of redemption"* (Ephesians 4:30 emphasis added)

Blessed assurance!

Finishing Strong

God's Blessings, Rewards, and Eternal Life for His Children

Our calendar rolled over into January 2004. Embracing challenges, Irad set a goal to run a marathon. Preparation was extreme—grueling physical and mental conditioning, rain or shine, every day.

Nine months later, October 2004 arrived. In great anticipation, we traveled to the Chicago Marathon. Sara, Irad's sister, joined us. She and her husband, Bill, arranged exquisite accommodations for us on the seventy-third floor of the John Hancock Building. We were set. On the night before the race, with dinner finished, when we were ready for sleep, the unexpected occurred. Irad developed excruciating back pain. He had bent over to check his watch and could not straighten. No preamble. It *just* happened.

We saw his goal sinking fast and called on the name of the Lord.

The travel bag emergency kit produced a muscle relaxer. We tried that, but the next morning, race day, he was no better.

Irad insisted that Sara and I take him to the start gate. We left him there with thirty thousand other runners. In that crowd, it was almost impossible to find a runner over a 26.2-mile distance.

Sara and I took the subway in an attempt to reach mile 13 ahead of the runners. Misrouted and miles away, we found a taxi, which brought us close; then we ran to mile 13. The racers were already coming through. We stood watching, as minutes passed. Had we missed Irad or was he in the race at all? Then we spotted him—*running like a thoroughbred*!

Irad achieved his goal that day—26.2 miles. He succeeded in finishing strong; he was awarded a medal.

The Lord desires that *all* run the race.

> Do you not know that those who run in a race all run, but *only* one receives the prize? Run in such a way that you may win. Everyone who competes in the games exercises self-control in all things. They then *do it* to receive a perishable wreath, but we an imperishable. Therefore I run in such a way, as not without aim; I box in such a way, as not beating the air; but I discipline my body and make it my slave, so that, after I have preached to others, I myself will not be disqualified. (1 Corinthians 9:24–27)

The Lord wants us to finish strong and be awarded the prize.

> I have fought a good fight, I have finished my course, I have kept the faith: Henceforth there is laid up for me a crown of righteousness, which the Lord, the righteous judge, shall give me at that day. (2 Timothy 4:7–8)

Because He Lives

God's Promise of Life to Those Who Believe

There are moments in time when a phone call bears the worst of news. My husband, Irad, took the call. Our fifth grandchild, nine-year-old Lydia, had been struck by a truck.

We were three minutes away from the scene of the accident. Upon arrival, we were directed to her. Lydia had been picked up from the pavement. Triage was underway in the ambulance. When I entered the ambulance, the picture of Lydia's face covered in blood was alarming. Not knowing the extent of her injuries, I went to her to provide reassurance.

When she realized I was at her side, with a piercing look, she asked a poignant question: "Am I going to die?"

Many people experiencing sickness or distress wonder the same.

Scripture teaches that we were born dying but that through Christ, believers begin living.

"We know that we have passed from death to life, because we love each other. Anyone who does not love remains in death" (1 John 3:14 NIV).

Lydia continues to live on earth, a vibrant young lady walking in faith. She is living her legacy of life — a legacy that begins on earth for those who believe in Jesus Christ as their Lord and Savior.

"Very truly I tell you, whoever hears my word and believes him who sent me has eternal life and will not be judged but has crossed over from death to life" (John 5:24 NIV).

Set in Stone

God's Promise for Eternal Life through Jesus Christ

Daddy finally achieved one of his dreams in 1985. He had always planned a small family lake on the farm. Cows were not allowed to trample the edges. The stocked pond was for beauty and pure enjoyment.

A simple pleasure was skipping stones across the lake. Irad is the family's record-holding stone skipper! He would choose a flat smooth stone, and his throw would skip—six, eight, ten times. Our children learned from the best and have won the family's amateur accolades for their prowess.

My stone would sink straight to the bottom!

Sinking stone warnings are recorded in Scripture.

"And whoever receives one such child in My name receives Me; but whoever causes one of these little ones who believe in Me to stumble, it would be better for him to have a heavy millstone hung around his neck, and to be drowned in the depth of the sea" (Matthew 18:5–7).

And yet, the Bible records stones in victory. Remember David as a shepherd boy? One stone brought down Goliath (see 1 Samuel 17).

There is an even greater *stone victory* in Scripture. One for obedience—engraved in love, and given to believers in Jesus Christ.

"Therefore, laying aside all malice, all deceit, hypocrisy, envy, and all evil speaking, as newborn babes, desire the pure milk of the word, that you may grow thereby, if indeed you have tasted that the Lord *is* gracious" (2 Peter 2:1–3 NKJV).

Jesus is the Chosen Stone and we are His chosen people. God's promised assurances are recorded in 1 Peter 2:4–6 (NKJV):

> Coming to Him as to a living stone, rejected indeed by men, but chosen by God and precious, you also, as living stones, are being built up a spiritual house, a holy priesthood, to offer up spiritual sacrifices acceptable to God through Jesus Christ. Therefore it is also contained in the Scripture,

> "Behold, I lay in Zion A chief cornerstone, elect, precious, And he who believes on Him will by no means be put to shame."

A New Name

God's Victory and Plan for the Ages

Every grandparent gets to choose a grandparent name by which to be called. I love having a *grand* name!

Our family grandparent names include Mamaw, Papaw, Grandma, Grandpa, Granny, and Nanaw (Nanaw was also called Hunk by her grandchildren, but *that is* another story).

Irad chose Granddaddy and I chose Grandy.

I wonder which names Jesus spoke when He addressed His earthly grandparents? Scripture does not tell us.

In days to come, members of the family of God, believers in the name of Jesus, will once again receive a new name—a name *grander* than ever, because Jesus Himself will name us.

> He who overcomes, I will make him a pillar in the temple of My God, and he will not go out from it anymore; and I will write on him the name of My God, and the name of the city of My God, the new Jerusalem, which comes down out of heaven from My God, and My new name. (Revelation 3:12)

Until that day, remember the Lord's promise written in Hebrews 13:20–21 (NIV),

> Now may the God of peace, who through the blood of the eternal covenant brought back from the dead our Lord Jesus, that great Shepherd of the sheep, equip you with everything good for doing his will, and may he work in us what is pleasing to him, through Jesus Christ, to whom be glory forever and ever. Amen.

Afterword: The Swan Song

God's Legacy of Life for His Children

There is one more story to tell. It is the condensed message of *Living the Legacy*, and it is most important in our time.

The world is changing at a rapid pace. There are wars and rumors of war, increased earthquake activity, intensified Christian persecution, a world fallen into lawlessness, and apostasy in the Church.

Jesus called the events birth pangs. Any woman who has birthed a child will testify that labor pains come quicker as the day of delivery approaches.

The Lord further described the occurrences we are witnessing as perilous. He urges us to be on the alert and be ready for His return.

Israel is established as a nation of the world (the fig tree has leafed out). The people of this generation are witnesses to the milestone. The Word of God advises us to recognize that His return is near: right at the door (Matthew 24).

Writing a book was never on my bucket list. The Father had different plans for me; and blazed upon my heart His message that I should add my voice to many others in warning.

If a people are warned, then how should they prepare for the Lord's coming?

The Swan Song story is my way of explaining. Here's how it goes.

Daddy was the last of our parents to leave for heaven.

Through Daddy's last will and testament, he left my sisters and me the inheritance of his beloved land.

After his funeral, we drove over the farm, as was Daddy's custom every single day. As we approached our small family lake, from a distance there appeared to be ten white trumpet swans.

A closer inspection revealed that the ten white birds were not swans but great egrets—five couples—which were nesting near the water for the first time ever.

Ten. The exact number of Daddy's family; five daughters and their husbands — five couples. We saw it as a message of reassurance from the Lord in our sadness.

At the end of that spring in 1998, the great white egrets left, never to reappear. I thanked the Lord for remembering my family by sending the beautiful white birds.

Later we realized that it was implausible to have ever been visited by trumpet swans, whose habitat is the Northwest, not the Southeast. While the egrets' visit was wonderful, a swan visit would have been thrilling, too.

Trumpet swans, endowed with grace and beauty, make the sound of a French horn, hence the name. The ancient Greeks believed that right before they die, trumpet swans break out in beautiful song.

Though I could not hear the song of the hearts of our departed family members, their time on earth was lived in harmony with the Lord, clothed in white robes of righteousness. They touched my life with special moments.

I'm frequently reminded of their essence in subtle ways: a melody, a favorite recipe, a turn of phrase, or the sound of someone's voice.

In the future, my family and all believers will hear the sound of the Lord's shout and the trumpet song as He reunites us once again.

"For the Lord Himself will descend from heaven with a shout, with the voice of the archangel and with the trumpet of God, and the dead in Christ will rise first. Then we who are alive and remain will be caught up together with them in the clouds to meet the Lord in the air, and so we shall always be with the Lord" (1 Thessalonians 4:16–17).

Faith in Jesus as Messiah is essential in preparation for that day when believers in Christ Jesus receive their inheritance, "which *is* imperishable and undefiled and will not fade away, reserved in heaven" (1 Peter 1:4).

"For whatever is born of God overcomes the world; and this is the victory that has overcome the world—our faith. Who is the one who overcomes the world, but he who believes that Jesus is the Son of God?" (1 John 5:4–5).

The Father's last will and testament has been written and made public. If you have not read His will, don't delay. The Bible reveals that through the death and resurrection of our Savior, Jesus Christ, all believers are named in God's will.

King David knew that he was named in God's will when David proclaimed, "In the scroll of the book it is written of me. I delight to do Your will, O my God; Your Law is within my heart" (Psalm 40:7–8).

The Father desires to adopt us into His family and to convey His legacy of life with Jesus forever.

"He who overcomes will inherit these things, and I will be his God and he will be My son" (Revelation 21:7).

Decisions are made every day: which school to attend, where to work, when to retire.

Time is fleeting. The Lord's return is drawing nigh. The most imperative decision of all is to surrender to Jesus Christ.

Be ready for His coming by strengthening your faith in study of His Word, brace to be an overcomer (to hold fast our faith in persecution and even unto death), and pray to be counted worthy of our calling.

The Father has promised that when we surrender to Jesus, he will deliver us. He will endow us with grace and beauty, fashion us for glory, and inspire our swan song of praise.

"He put a new song in my mouth, a song of praise to our God; Many will see and fear, And will trust in the Lord." (Psalm 40:3)

The Lee Family Album

Memories of Days Gone By

"So these days were to be remembered and celebrated throughout every generation, every family, every province and every city..." Esther 9:28

"Fly'n High"
Above left: Irad and Jean Lee prepare for departure following a
weeklong Acapulco vacation; *above right:* Hyatt Regency,
Acapulco, Mexico, 1978

"I Want to Hold Your Hand"
Jean Lee with her daddy, R.S. (Prof)
Howard

"Love at First Sight"
Home at Legacy Springs,
Rachel Lee and her grandy,
Jean Lee

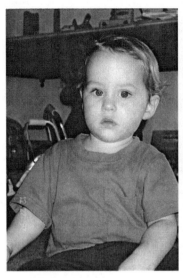

"The Tracks of His Tears"
Irad Lee IV, at age three,
1999

"Splash"
Left to right: Dean Denton and Jean Lee
at Houston Park Pool

"Take the Bull by the Horns"
Above left: R.S. (Prof) Howard pictured years after
the bull gored him; *above right:* The barn built in
1939 at the Howard Farm still stands today

"The Giant Slayer"
Annalee Rogers movie watching with
grandaddy, Irad Lee

"No Bull"
Irad Lee at work on
Daddy's farm, 1998

"Everything's Coming Up Roses"
Jean Lee's sisters, *left to right*: Jean Lee, Dean Denton, Pat Herrell,
Nancy Tilley, Linda Heiskell

"Tears on My Pillow"
Mother's Day, 1997, Angelia Crawley Lee; infant son,
Irad Lee IV; and husband, Irad Lee III

"Playing Hardball"
Irad Lee Sr.

"Sign Language"
Thirteen years old in 2011, Katherine
Haymes at our home with her cousin,
Irad Lee IV

"Family Jewels"
Irad Lee's brother and sisters at the hospital, Destin Florida, 1989, *left to right*: Barbara Pennington, Sara Orman, David Lee, Ann Barlette, Janie Lee, Irad Lee

"Fish Out of Water"
Madi Haymes at age 12

"Praise to the Skies"
Left to right: Mary Blake and Katherine Howard, Jordan Family Reunion in Dayton, Tennessee, 1956

"Love You to the Dump"
Julia Lee Rogers and daughter,
Annalee Rogers

"By the Book"
Alton and Jewel Eddleman

"A Family Tradition"
Prom night 2015; *front center:* Annalee Rogers, *left to right:* Madi
Haymes, Julia Lee Rogers, Katherine Haymes, Lydia Haymes

"Bridging the Gap"
Katherine Howard at roadside
picnic 1957

"I Want to Go Home"
Walter and Hattie Howard at
home with a great-grandson,
Sale Creek, Tennessee

"War and Peace"
Above left: Irad Lee; *above right from left to right,* Jean Lee and Sara
Orman; All are making "sad faces" just for fun as they return home
from their trip to the Gulf Coast, 1988

"The Bucket List"
Georgie Lee at her stove, 1969

"Finishing Strong"
Irad Lee finishes Chicago
Marathon, 2004

"Because He Lives"
Above left: Lydia Haymes at nine years old after her accident, 2012;
above right: Lydia and her granddaddy, Irad Lee, enjoying time
together, 2013

Jean Lee's parents	Irad Lee's parents
R.S. (Prof) and Katherine Howard	Irad Lee Sr. and Georgie (Hunk) Lee

The Howard Family
Family lake day 2011 at the home of Jim and Linda Heiskell

Irad and Jean Lee's son-in-law
and daughter
Shawn and Julia Lee Rogers

Irad and Jean Lee's son and
granddaughter
Irad Lee III and Rachel Lee

Irad and Jean Lee's grandchildren, at their home on Easter Sunday, 2015
Left to right: Katherine Haymes, Lydia Haymes, Madi Haymes,
Rachel Lee, Annalee Rogers, Irad Lee IV

Irad and Jean Lee's children
Julia Lee Rogers and Irad Lee III

Irad and Jean Lee

CPSIA information can be obtained at www.ICGtesting.com
Printed in the USA
LVOW11s0018040915

452606LV00001B/2/P